HOW TO FORM

A

NONPROFIT

CORPORATION

How to Form a Nonprofit Corporation

Third Edition

Mark Warda
Attorney at Law

SPHINX® PUBLISHING
AN IMPRINT OF SOURCEBOOKS, INC.®
NAPERVILLE, ILLINOIS
www.SphinxLegal.com

Third Edition, 2004

Published by: **Sphinx® Publishing, An Imprint of Sourcebooks, Inc.®**

Naperville Office
P.O. Box 4410
Naperville, Illinois 60567-4410
630-961-3900
Fax: 630-961-2168
www.sourcebooks.com
www.SphinxLegal.com

This publication is designed to provide accurate and authoritative information in regard to the subject matter covered. It is sold with the understanding that the publisher is not engaged in rendering legal, accounting, or other professional service. If legal advice or other expert assistance is required, the services of a competent professional person should be sought.

From a Declaration of Principles Jointly Adopted by a Committee of the
American Bar Association and a Committee of Publishers and Associations

This product is not a substitute for legal advice.

Disclaimer required by Texas statutes.

Library of Congress Cataloging-in-Publication Data
Warda, Mark.
  How to form a nonprofit corporation / by Mark Warda.-- 3rd ed.
     p. cm.
  Includes index.
  ISBN 1-57248-390-3 (alk. paper)
  1. Nonprofit organizations--Law and legislation--United
States--Popular works. 2. Incorporation--United States--Popular works.
3. Nonprofit organizations--Law and legislation--United States--Forms.
4. Incorporation--United States--Forms. I. Title.
KF1388.Z9 W37 2004
346.73'064--dc22
                                            200402461

Printed and bound in the United States of America.

VHG — 10 9 8 7 6 5 4 3 2 1

CONTENTS

INTRODUCTION

The nonprofit organization is a particularly American institution. As early as the 1830s, political and social observationist Alexis de Tocqueville remarked that Americans were "constantly forming associations." Today, the United States has the most advanced system of nonprofit organizations in the world. Americans often rely on each other and are eager to volunteer when needed to improve society and show the independent spirit that has always influenced this country.

Over a million nonprofit organizations exist in the country. Nonprofit organizations make up over twelve percent of the economy. They are estimated to control nearly two trillion dollars in assets. As our society becomes wealthier, we can expect many more nonprofit organizations to form.

Whether you have enough money to fund a nonprofit organization yourself or plan to rely on the generosity of others, the nonprofit corporation is the best vehicle for aiding a cause in which you believe. Whether you seek a cure for cancer or just closer ties among your ethnic group, the nonprofit corporation can help you claim all the benefits given to such organizations and establish something that can continue forever.

The benefits of nonprofit status are numerous. The best known benefit is the tax-free status. Nonprofits also enjoy lower postage rates, discounts from some businesses, lower governmental fees, the ability to qualify for private and government grants, and free air time or ads by some media outlets. Many nonprofits can attract funds from taxpayers because donations to the organizations are deductible.

You can show that you have another American trait—the do-it-yourself entrepreneurial spirit—by using this book. Rather than hire a lawyer, you can do a lot of the work yourself and save a lot of money to put toward your cause. However, you should realize that the law of nonprofit organizations is complicated. There are a lot of strict government rules that must be followed in order to qualify for all of the benefits. In some situations, you may need to pay for expert advice to be sure you have done everything right. The most complicated areas are noted in the text and you are advised when legal guidance may be necessary.

Fortunately, many organizations exist whose purpose is to help other nonprofits. Also, a wealth of information about nonprofit organizations can be found on the Internet. (Perhaps too much—a recent search turned up over a million sites.) We have found some of the best sites and refer to them throughout the text.

Good luck with your organization!

I DEFINITION OF A NONPROFIT ORGANIZATION

A *nonprofit organization* is one that does not pass its income to its members or shareholders, but instead uses the income to further a goal that benefits the community or some part of the community.

This does not mean that the operations of a nonprofit cannot be profitable. Many nonprofit organizations make large profits on their operations, but those profits cannot benefit private parties. They must be used to further the organization's stated goal. If a nonprofit disbands, no one except another qualified nonprofit organization (with goals as similar as possible) can take over its assets.

Advantages of Nonprofit Status

There are four main advantages of being a nonprofit organization rather than an ordinary business: the tax exemptions; the ability to receive tax-deductible donations; the ability to qualify for grants; and, the lower costs for such things as postage, advertising, and filing fees.

Tax Exemption For many nonprofits, the tax exemptions are the most important benefits. Several exemptions from taxes are available depending on the type of organization and the state in which it is located.

Income received by most nonprofits is not subject to income tax at either the state or federal level if they successfully apply for and are granted an *exemption*. In most states, nonprofits can get an exemption from paying sales and use taxes on items that the organization purchases. Also, many nonprofits do not have to pay property taxes on the real estate they own. Again, they must apply for, and be granted, the exemption.

Deductibility of Contributions

Perhaps more important than being tax exempt, contributions made by taxpayers to certain types of nonprofits are *deductible* on the taxpayer's income tax return. This is a big incentive for others to give to an organization. Without this deduction, many nonprofits would not survive. (The laws about soliciting donations are covered in Chapter 6.)

Grants

Being a nonprofit organization makes your group eligible for both private and government grants. There are many large foundations that are required by law to give away a percentage of their assets each year, but they can only do so to qualified nonprofit organizations. (Applying for grants is discussed in Chapter 6.)

Lower Costs

The postal service offers special rates to nonprofit organizations that are much lower than the normal rates. Some newspapers, magazines, radio stations, and other media give discounted advertising rates to nonprofits. In some cases it is even possible for nonprofit organizations to advertise for free. These advertisements are known as *public service announcements*.

Tax-Exempt Bonds

Some types of nonprofit organizations are able to raise money by issuing tax-exempt bonds, which are similar to municipal bonds. This is usually done by organizations that need to finance multi-million dollar facilities, like hospitals.

Disadvantages of Nonprofit Status

The benefits of nonprofit status would be useful to nearly all types of businesses and organizations. Many businesses could successfully operate as nonprofits. But there are also disadvantages that make many types of organizations unable to operate as nonprofits. In recent years, some for-profit businesses complained that nonprofits were competing against them unfairly. So the laws have been changed to make it more difficult for nonprofits to engage in activities that compete with for-profit businesses.

One of the most important things to know about a nonprofit organization is that it is not *owned* by its founders. Unlike a private business that can be sold after it has grown big and profitable, a nonprofit organization *belongs* to the public at large. If it dissolves, its assets must be given to another nonprofit organization that has a stated business purpose that is as similar as possible to the dissolved nonprofit's purpose. If its assets are misapplied or used for private benefit by the officers, the state attorney general (or a similar official) can seize them.

Loss of Control

If you are planning to put a lot of money and time into an organization, you should consider whether the advantages are worth the loss of control of the profits. However, there are ways to set up a nonprofit to give yourself *de facto* control and you are allowed to pay yourself a reasonable salary and set up a pension plan. The limits on these are discussed later in the book.

Limited Purposes

In order to be exempt under the tax laws, a nonprofit organization can only perform certain functions listed in those laws. If it goes outside those limits, the nonprofit may have to pay taxes on some of its income, pay penalties, or lose its exemption entirely.

Lobbying

Most types of tax-exempt, nonprofit organizations are forbidden from contributing to political campaigns and may only do a limited amount of lobbying. (This is discussed in more detail in Chapter 5.)

Public Scrutiny

Another disadvantage is public scrutiny. Because a nonprofit organization is dedicated to the public, its finances are open to public inspection. This means that the public can obtain copies of any nonprofit's tax returns and find out its salaries and other expenditures.

Laws that Apply to Nonprofit Organizations

There are three main sets of laws that apply to nonprofit organizations. *State corporation laws* control the formation and operation of the organization. *State charitable solicitation laws* control the activities of the organization if it is soliciting donations from the public. *Federal tax laws* govern which organizations can qualify as tax exempt and which activities may be undertaken by tax exempt organizations.

State Laws   State corporation laws cover the formation of the nonprofit corporation. They set the requirements for the *articles of organization*, the procedures for amendments, and the other structural and operational issues.

A summary of each state's laws is included in Appendix B. You can use this summary to get an idea of how your organization can be formed and how it will be regulated. However, you should also obtain copies of the statutes themselves. In running your organization, you will want to be sure not to violate any of them.

State charitable solicitation laws regulate organizations that solicit money from the public and are designed to protect consumers from fraud. There have been numerous cases in which organizations have claimed to be collecting money to fight cancer or feed the hungry, but actually have kept most of the money for themselves.

Not all states regulate charitable solicitation and each of the states that do have different requirements. Whether a state has regulations or any exemptions, the addresses to write to are in Appendix B. (More information on the requirements is in Chapter 6.)

Federal   Federal tax laws are far more important than state laws. The federal tax laws con-
Tax Laws   trol what a nonprofit may or may not do if it wishes to take advantage of the tax exemptions.

State laws are usually very broad and allow nonprofits wide leeway in their purposes. Nearly any small group that does not intend to distribute its profit to its members could easily fall under the nonprofit law of most states. However, federal tax laws applicable to nonprofits are very strict and sometimes contradictory and confusing. Consider the following situations.

   ✪   Because rich donors were setting up nonprofits to hire their family members and avoid estate taxes, a law was passed saying that nonprofits were forbidden to benefit private parties (the *private inurement* doctrine). But what about nonprofit social clubs whose sole purpose is to benefit their members? Well, they can only benefit their members and not serve the public.

   ✪   Because the government does not give tax benefits to groups that discriminate, nonprofits are forbidden from discriminating on the basis of race, religion, etc. But what about religious nonprofit organizations? Well, they can discriminate on the basis of religion if they have a good reason.

✪   To be sure the government does not subsidize groups that support those who hold office, nonprofits are not allowed to contribute to political campaigns. However, they can set up *political action committees* (PACs) that are also nonprofit organizations, but contribute to political campaigns as their *sole purpose.*

Every year the IRS issues new Revenue Rulings, the courts issue new opinions, and usually Congress tinkers with the law. How can you ever hope to comply with such a system? Keep in mind that the people enforcing the law are no more intelligent than you, and in many cases they are as confused as you.

So here is your best strategy.

✪   Learn as much about the laws as you can and make a good faith effort to follow them carefully. If you are planning something that might be questionable, ask a tax specialist for an opinion.

✪   Keep good records.

✪   If your tax return or activities are questioned, make it clear that you are doing your best to comply and cooperate fully. (But get the best tax advice you can afford to be sure of your rights.)

Other Laws   Other than the specific laws for nonprofits, most laws that apply to other businesses also apply to nonprofits. In most states, for example, the general rules for business corporation procedures apply to nonprofit corporations. Federal election laws apply to nonprofit corporations as well as business corporations.

Permitted Purposes

A nonprofit organization may be formed for any legal purpose under most state laws, as long as it does not pass its profits on to its members. But in order to qualify for favorable tax treatment and gain other benefits, it must limit its purposes to those allowed in the *Internal Revenue Code* (I.R.C.). The following are some of the most popular purposes allowed by the law.

**Section
501 (c)(3)
Organizations**

The best tax treatment is available to nonprofits that qualify under Section 501(c)(3) of the I.R.C. These organizations get both a tax exemption and the ability for their contributors to deduct contributions. Permitted purposes under this section include the following.

Religious. Religion is the oldest and broadest category of nonprofit. Because the First Amendment to the Constitution bars the government from making any law that prohibits the free exercise of religion, the government is limited in how much it can regulate religious activities. However, some courts have required newly formed religious groups to be similar to traditional religions, with such things as an established congregation, an organized ministry, regular services, education of the young, and a doctrinal code in order for them to qualify for a tax exemption. This was done to keep people from setting up their own religions just for tax purposes.

Charitable. Under the tax law, the word *charitable* is broader than the normal definition of relieving poverty. Court decisions over the years have allowed all of the following activities to be undertaken by organizations that qualify for Section 501(c)(3) status.

- ✪ *Relieving poverty.* Any activity that gives aid to the poor, such as soup kitchens or homeless shelters, may qualify. But it must direct its benefit to the public at large and not to any particular person. For example, a group that forms to help a particular family that loses its home in a fire will not qualify for tax exempt status. To qualify, its purpose would have to be to help all fire victims in a certain area.

- ✪ *Beautifying the community.* Groups that plant trees and clean up highways can qualify for charitable status. The limitation is that they must serve a broad community such as a city or town. If they only serve a limited number of people, such as a subdivision, they will not qualify.

- ✪ *Lessening the burdens of government.* Groups that help existing government programs, through activities such as improving parks or police facilities, are included as charitable organizations.

- ✪ *Promoting health.* Hospitals, blood banks, clinics, mental health organizations, and groups with similar functions all qualify for charitable status as long as their profits do not go to private individuals.

✪ *Promoting social welfare.* Groups that promote social welfare are groups that support civil rights, community alliance, national defense, or similar causes.

✪ *Promoting environmental conservation.* Groups that work to preserve national resource may qualify as promoting environmental conservation.

✪ *Promoting the arts.* Groups that sponsor arts festivals, theater groups, concerts, and programs to encourage young people to develop their talents are covered.

✪ *Promoting patriotism.* Groups that participate in patriotic displays and *inculcate patriotic emotions* are considered groups that promote patriotism.

✪ *Promoting amateur sports.* Groups that support amateur sports such as little leagues and soccer clubs, but not simply any group that provides athletic facilities or equipment, may qualify as a charitable organization.

Scientific. Scientific research that is theoretical is clearly allowable for charitable nonprofit organizations, but research that is practical and has business applications is not. Testing products is not considered charitable (unless done for public safety) and doing work for one particular company is clearly not allowed.

Testing for public safety. Organizations like Underwriters Laboratories, Inc., which test the safety of products, are tax exempt.

Literary. Literary organizations are exempt if their work is not commercial, but rather promotes the literacy of the community. For example, a publisher that sells books at normal prices will probably not qualify, but one that sells the works of unknown talented people at a discount price may qualify.

Educational. Educational organizations can include libraries and museums as well as traditional schools, colleges, and universities. For the tax exemption, it is important that the school is an objective place of learning rather than a promoter of a particular idea.

Preventing cruelty to children or animals. Organizations like the Society for the Prevention of Cruelty to Animals (SPCA), orphanages, or any group that aids children or animals are included, as long as the group is not limited to any particular child or animal.

The IRS uses two tests to determine if an organization qualifies under Section 501(c)(3)—the *organizational test* and the *operational test*. Under the *organizational test*, the documentation that forms the organization must limit the organization's purpose and activities to those that are permitted. For this reason, it is very important that the articles of incorporation and the bylaws are carefully drafted to pass IRS examination.

Under the *operational test*, the operations or activities must also comply with the law. It is not enough that the paperwork of the organization is correct—the organization must also conduct itself in conformance with those rules.

If the purpose or activities of a nonprofit organization do not qualify for an exemption under Section 501(c)(3), it still may claim an exemption under one of the other subsections of 501(c). The disadvantage is that under most of the other subsections, the income is tax exempt, but contributions may *not* be deducted on donors' tax returns.

Other Types of Organizations

The rationale for other types of tax-exempt organizations is completely different from Section 501(c)(3) organizations. While Section 501(c)(3) organizations are exempt because they are perceived to be doing something beneficial to society, these others are not taxed because they are pooling money to do something that would not be taxed if the money were not pooled.

For example, if a number of people use their money to lobby for better roads or to socialize every Sunday night, there is no tax involved. So if they put their money together in an organization to do the same thing, there is no reason they should have to pay an extra tax on that money.

The problem arises when these groups try to raise money from outside sources. If a social club charges its members ten dollars for dinner, but charges outside guests twenty dollars for the same dinner, then the members who pay less are making a *profit* on the arrangement. This type of activity by a nonprofit organization is subject to tax.

Some organizations divide their operations into two or more nonprofit organizations. For example, a Section 501(c)(3) organization may have a *subsidiary* under another 501(c) subsection to perform activities forbidden under Section 501(c)(3) rules.

The following are some of the most common tax exempt organizations under categories other than Section 501(c)(3).

Civic and social welfare associations. An organization can be formed under Section 501(c)(4) to promote the common good and social welfare of a community. You could use this type of organization if you wanted to do something forbidden to 501(c)(3) organizations, such as lobby for better roads or schools. Because contributions to these organizations are not deductible, you should try to fit your purpose into a Section 501(c)(3) by concentrating on permitted purposes, and only form under Section 501(c)(4) if that is impossible.

Employee associations. Also under Section 501(c)(4), an association of employees of one employer can be formed if their net earnings are devoted exclusively to charitable, educational, or recreational purposes.

Labor organizations. A labor or agricultural worker organization can be formed under Section 501(c)(5) if the goal is to improve conditions, production, or efficiency.

Trade associations. Groups that promote the common interest of a business community or a line of businesses, such as a chamber of commerce or board of real estate, are exempt under Section 501(c)(6). However, the group may not carry on business itself. It may only promote the interests of all businesses in the same field.

The trade association must be involved with only one trade. If it is a group of people from different trades who meet to network, it will not qualify under Section 501(c)(6), though it may be able to qualify as a social club or other type of exempt organization. It must allow competitors in the same field to be members—it cannot support only one faction of an industry.

Social clubs. A club that is formed solely for pleasure and recreational purposes is exempt under Section 501(c)(7) if most of its income is from member dues and only an insubstantial amount is raised from the public.

With the strict rules that a nonprofit organization cannot give any benefits to its members, it seems anomalous that a group whose sole purpose is to benefit its members could qualify. But as explained before, there is no reason to tax groups that merely pool their money to do something that would not be taxed if paid for separately.

In order to qualify as a tax exempt social club, an organization must have a membership that commingles and has shared interests. Some groups that have qualified are fraternities and sororities, lunch and dinner clubs, golf and tennis clubs, gem collectors, large families, and political clubs. One organization that was disallowed an exemption was an auto club because the IRS found that the interests of the members were too different.

Cemeteries. If a cemetery is not designed to make a profit, but instead to provide plots exclusively for its members, it can be tax exempt under Section 501(c)(13).

Veterans' organizations. If seventy-five percent of the members of a veterans' organization are past or present members of the armed forces and most of the rest are relatives of veterans, it can qualify as tax exempt under Section 501(c)(19).

Prohibited Practices

There are certain activities nonprofit organizations are prohibited from doing. Violation of these rules can cause the loss of tax-exempt status or even penalties and fines.

Many of these rules were enacted when nonprofit organizations were accused of abusing their status. When one nonprofit opposed the re-election of a United States senator, a law was passed to prohibit them from political activities. When some rich families began using nonprofit organizations to employ family members, laws were passed to prohibit such arrangements. Every few years, someone does an exposé of abuses at nonprofits and new laws are proposed to control these organizations. As a nonprofit organization, your group will want to keep abreast of proposals for changes in the law.

There are big differences in what charitable (Section 501(c)(3)) groups can do (those that can collect tax deductible contributions) and what other nonprofits can do. The limits are much more strict for charitable groups because the deductibility of their income is considered a government subsidy that should go to the good of the community rather than to a few individuals.

The following are the major prohibitions for nonprofit organizations.

No Specific Benefit

For nonprofit organizations to qualify as charitable, the focus of their mission must be the community at large, not any individual or small group of individuals. For example, you can get an exemption for a group that wants to aid tornado victims, but not for a group formed to help one specific victim. Similarly, you can get an exemption to clean up an entire community, but not just one subdivision.

Groups that do benefit limited numbers of people, such as social clubs, trade groups, and homeowners associations, can be nonprofit and tax exempt, but the members' dues are not deductible and their outside income must be limited.

No Private Inurement

Similar to the requirement that the purpose of the nonprofit be to aid the community, the *private inurement doctrine* does not allow private parties to receive *undue profits* from a nonprofit organization.

This means that the organizer and directors cannot get inflated salaries or other unusual financial arrangements. Business dealings between a nonprofit and persons related to it are put under careful scrutiny and can result in penalties or loss of tax exemption if found to be unreasonable.

Business dealings are allowed between nonprofits and their members and directors, but they should be at commercially reasonable terms. For example, if an organization rents an office from one if its directors, the rent should be documented as fair and reasonable. If the rent is inflated, the organization's tax status is in jeopardy.

In the real world, nonprofits get away with a lot more than the law books would have you believe. Exposés by such publications as *U.S.News & World Report* and the *Philadelphia Inquirer* uncovered nonprofit officers making hundreds of thousands—even millions—of dollars in salaries, guaranteed loans, and numerous other alleged abuses.

Limited Lobbying

Because of perceived abuses, Congress has put strict restraints on the types of lobbying that can be done by charitable organizations. However, no such limits apply to nonprofit organizations that are *not charitable*.

Charitable nonprofits. Charitable nonprofit organizations (those whose contributions are deductible) are prohibited from contributing to political campaigns and their lobbying cannot be substantial. Private foundations cannot lobby at all and other charitable organizations must stick to certain limits. The exact limits are determined by applying either the *expenditures test* or the *substantial part test*. (These tests are explained in more detail in Chapter 5.)

Other nonprofits. Nonprofits that are not charitable (social welfare associations, trade associations, social clubs, labor unions) are free to lobby as long as the lobbying is related to their specific organizational goal. However, if the dues of members are used for lobbying, then that amount may not be deducted as a business expense (or in any other way) by the members.

Political organizations. Organizations that are formed to support particular political candidates can be nonprofits and give unlimited amounts to campaigns, but they are not allowed to lobby to influence legislation because it is not part of their exempt function, namely supporting particular candidates.

Limited Commercial Activities

Because of complaints by businesses that they cannot compete with tax exempt organizations that are in the same business, nonprofit organizations are limited in the types of commercial activities in which they can engage. If a nonprofit does engage in a business venture that is unrelated to its purpose, the profits from that venture are taxable. But if a nontaxable organization has too much taxable income, it may lose its tax exempt status. For this reason, successful nonprofit groups such as the National Geographic Society, have had to spin off operations that became too profitable.

There are some loopholes nonprofits can use to make money and still avoid paying taxes. These include selling donated items, performing services provided by volunteers, and giving away small items. (For more details about this information, see Chapter 5.)

2 | CHOOSING A TYPE OF NONPROFIT ORGANIZATION

Before forming a nonprofit organization, you should understand the types of structures available so that you can choose the one that will provide the most benefits to the type of organization you are planning.

Association, Trust, or Corporation

A nonprofit organization can organize itself in three ways—as an unincorporated association, a trust, or a corporation. For most groups, a corporation offers the most advantages, but in certain situations, the others may work better.

Association   Any informal group of people who get together for a common purpose, such as a bridge club, Parent Teacher Association, or a ski club, can be considered an *unincorporated association*. Such a group has some legal rights, like the right to open a bank account. However, this structure has some legal liabilities. For example, if the members of a ski club are driving together and get into an accident because of the negligence of the member driving, it is possible that all members of the club could be liable to the person injured, whether or not that person is a club member. For this reason, groups that are involved in risky activities are advised to incorporate.

Small groups of friends who do things together usually do not have to worry, since their auto and homeowners' insurance will cover most possible risks. But if the group expands beyond a small group of friends, starts generating income, or wishes to apply for grants or deductible donations, it should incorporate for the advantages listed under the corporation section.

Trust

A few types of nonprofit organizations are more often formed as *trusts*. For example, charitable gifts made in wills are often set up as charitable trusts. Also, political committees are set up as trusts because federal election laws prohibit corporations from giving money to political campaigns. Multi-employer pension plans must be set up as trusts, as are many other pension plans.

However, for most groups that have members this is not a good entity, since the trustees are not protected against liability. In fact, *trustees* may have a greater exposure to liability because they are held to a higher, *fiduciary* standard. This means that they must be extremely careful in their dealings or they can be personally liable for their mistakes.

Corporation

The corporation is the most common, and usually best, form for a nonprofit organization. Some of the benefits are listed here.

Protection from liability. The officers, directors, and members of a nonprofit corporation are protected, in most cases, from liability for the debts and obligations of the corporation. If the corporation incurs debts or if someone is injured by a member of the corporation, the others in the organization normally will not be personally liable. There are exceptions to this, however. If the officers or members personally guarantee the debt or if they cause the injury, they will be held liable.

Eligibility for grants. Many government and private programs can only make grants to organizations that are incorporated.

Procedural rules. When an organization incorporates, it is then governed by state incorporation law. This law usually answers all of the issues that come up in such an organization, such as how many directors there must be, what is a valid *quorum*, and what are the rights of members. If the organization is unincorporated, it must make up its own procedures for all of these issues.

There is a price to pay for these benefits, but it is well worth it. The organization must register with a state and must make periodic filings and disclosures.

There are also filing fees, but these are usually small. If professionals are hired to prepare these documents, the cost may be high, but this is not necessary for small groups whose affairs are not complicated.

Domestic or Foreign

The first decision that must be made when forming a nonprofit corporation is whether it will be *domestic* (formed in the state in which it is operating) or *foreign* (formed in another state). In nearly all cases, it is best to form a domestic corporation. While the paperwork is about the same, for foreign corporations there is an extra registration fee and you must hire a registered agent in the state in which the foreign corporation is formed.

Reasons for Incorporating Out-of-State

There are two good reasons to use a foreign nonprofit corporation. First, you may wish to have less than three directors and your state may require three. Many nonprofits have more than three directors because this broadens support and looks better to those providing grants and to the IRS. But some people who intend to put a lot of their time and money into a new organization are not willing to share the power to make decisions. It may be possible to get friends or relatives to be the additional directors, but if this is not convenient, you could incorporate in a state that allows a single director.

The following states allow a single director in a nonprofit corporation:

✪ California	✪ Oklahoma
✪ Colorado	✪ Oregon
✪ Delaware	✪ Pennsylvania
✪ Iowa	✪ South Carolina
✪ Kansas	✪ Virginia
✪ Michigan	✪ Washington
✪ Mississippi	✪ West Virginia
✪ New Hampshire	

In New Hampshire and South Carolina, although nonprofits only need one director, multiple people need to sign the incorporation papers to start the organization (five in New Hampshire and two in South Carolina).

The second reason to use another state is to have a *stock-based* nonprofit corporation in a state that does not allow it. A stock-based nonprofit corporation is one that is controlled by its stockholders. This keeps the control of the organization in a limited number of persons. Of course, the stockholders cannot receive any dividends or profits of the organization.

Most states do not allow nonprofits to be set up as stock based, so to form one you need to set up the organization in a state that does. First check with your state to see if a stock-based nonprofit qualifies to do business there because in some states, they do.

Membership or Nonmembership

A nonprofit corporation must decide whether to have members, and if it does, if there will be different classes of members, such as voting and nonvoting.

Allowing people to become members of a nonprofit organization may seem like a good way to get support, but because formal members of nonprofits are granted legal rights to control it, many organizations decide against formal membership, at least in the beginning. In most states, formal members have a right to vote on major decisions and to choose directors or officers. This can be time consuming, costly, and it opens the risk that a splinter group may take over the organization. Consider, for example, if a group of concerned citizens organizes a group to fight the pollution of a chemical plant. If the plant asks all its employees to join the organization, they could become a majority and vote to disband it.

One way to keep control with a membership corporation is to provide that the officers and directors are elected from a slate chosen by a *nominating committee*. This committee can be composed of the founding members and those they approve.

However, the easiest way to keep control of a nonprofit corporation is to set it up as a nonmembership organization. The **BYLAWS** included in this book are for a nonmembership corporation. (see form 6, p.141) If you wish to have a membership organization, you can use the **ADDENDUM TO BYLAWS** or rewrite the **BYLAWS** to include those sections. (see form 7, p.147)

As an incentive to support an organization, you can give people an informal membership or list then as *benefactors*, *contributors*, *associates*, or a similar title. This gives them the feeling of being part of the organization without giving them the power to control its affairs.

Charitable or Noncharitable

The law of nonprofit organizations can be confusing because there are two meanings for the word *charitable*. One refers to a charity that, for example, aids the poor. The other refers to the broader IRS definition that includes all organizations that can accept tax-deductible contributions. These include educational, religious, scientific, patriotic, and many other types of organizations that are classified under Section 501(c)(3) of the Internal Revenue Code.

If at all possible, you should form your organization to comply with this section and therefore become a *charitable organization*. To do so, you must draft your *statement of purpose* to fit into the permitted purposes under the law. (This statement is explained in more detail in Chapter 4.)

If you cannot possibly fit your planned activities into a Section 501(c)(3) organization, such as if you plan to do substantial lobbying for new laws or to contribute to political campaigns, you can form a *noncharitable* nonprofit organization under one of the other exemptions. These include:

- ✪ business leagues (trade associations) under Section 501(c)(6);

- ✪ chambers of commerce under Section 501(c)(6);

- ✪ civic leagues under Section 501(c)(4);

- ✪ employee associations under Section 501(c)(4), (9), or (17);

- ✪ labor organizations under Section 501(c)(5);

- ✪ lodges under Section 501(c)(10);

- recreational clubs under Section 501(c)(7);

- social clubs under Section 501(c)(7);

- social welfare organizations under Section 501(c)(4); and,

- veterans' organizations under Section 501(c)(19).

Under these sections, an organization can be exempt from paying income taxes, but contributions given to it will not be tax deductible as charitable contributions. However, they might be tax deductible for another reason. For example, dues to a trade association are usually tax deductible for businesses in the same trade.

Public Charity or Private Foundation

If you are able to be a charitable organization under Section 501(c)(3), you must determine whether your organization is a *public charity* or a *private foundation*. Every nonprofit should endeavor to avoid private foundation status, since this status can result in some very difficult rules.

Public Charity

All new charitable organizations are presumed to be private foundations unless they can pass certain tests and become public charities. There are three ways to be classified as a public charity—qualifying automatically, passing the *public support test*, or passing the *facts and circumstances test*. These are spelled out in detail in IRS Publication 557 and are summarized below.

Automatic qualification. A charity automatically qualifies as public if it is one of the following types of organizations:

- a church;

- a school with formal instruction and a regularly enrolled student body;

- a hospital;

- a medical research facility;

✪ a public safety organization; or,

✪ an organization that supports one of the above.

Public support test. If a charity does not qualify automatically for public charity status, it can qualify if it receives broad public support. For this, the IRS requires an organization to receive at least one-third of its total financial support from public support sources, such as donations from the public.

Facts and circumstances test. If a charity cannot pass the public support test, there is a third way to qualify. First, it must receive at least ten percent of its funding as public support. Next, it must carry on *bona fide programs* to attract public support on a continual basis. Finally, the IRS will look at the following factors:

✪ the percentage of public support (10% or more needed);

✪ the sources of the support (not all from the same family);

✪ the makeup of the governing body (community leaders, government officials, clergy help);

✪ the benefits available to the public (rather than a select group) from the organization; and,

✪ the makeup of the membership and audience of the organization (broad audience is better).

An organization does not have to satisfy all of these factors, but the factors will be weighed depending on the nature of the organization.

Private Foundations

If a nonprofit organization cannot qualify for public charity status through any of the above tests, it will be classified as a private foundation. As a private foundation, it must comply with the rules under the I.R.C. It must:

✪ distribute its income each year so as not to be subject to Section 4942 tax;

✪ avoid any self-dealing as defined in Section 4941(d);

✪ avoid retaining business holdings as defined in Section 4943(c);

✪ refrain from any investments taxable under Section 4944;

✪ refrain from any expenditures as defined in Section 4945(d); and,

✪ pay an excise tax on its investment income.

Donors who give to a private foundation can only deduct up to thirty percent of their adjusted gross income, whereas for a public charity, they can deduct up to fifty percent.

Private operating foundations. If a private foundation can become classified as a *private operating foundation*, it can qualify for donors to be able to deduct up to fifty percent of their contributions, and it can be relieved of the requirement to distribute funds received from private foundations within one year. To qualify, it must meet the *asset test*, the *support test*, or the *endowment test*, and it must distribute eighty-five percent of its income each year.

Under the assets test, 65% or more of assets are devoted directly to exempt activity or a related business or consists of stock in a corporation that is 80% controlled by the foundation, and at least 85% of assets are devoted to exempt activity or related business. Under the support test, at least 85% of support comes from the general public; not more than 25% comes from one exempt organization and not more than 50% of support comes from investments. Under the endowment test, at least two-thirds of its minimum investment return is distributed directly for exempt functions. (Minimum investment return is 5% of excess of value of exempt assets over the indebtedness to acquire those assets.) (For more information, see IRS Publication 557.)

Exempt operating foundations. A third possibility for a private foundation is to qualify as an *exempt operating foundation*. As an exempt operating foundation, an organization does not have to pay the excise tax on net investment income. A private operating foundation can qualify as exempt if it has been publicly supported for at least ten years, has a governing body that broadly represents the public, and has no officers and no more than twenty-five percent of the governing board as *disqualified individuals* (major donors or their family members). (See IRS Publication 557 for more details.)

3 START-UP PROCEDURES

The first step in forming a nonprofit corporation, registering with the state, is explained in this chapter. The second step, obtaining your tax exemption is explained in the next chapter.

Send for Forms and Instructions

The first thing to do to form a nonprofit corporation is obtain the forms and instructions that are available from your state's corporate registration office (usually the Secretary of State). Some states provide a lot of information, others only the basics. Some are available over the Internet, some by mail. (Refer to your state in Appendix B for more details.)

If you ask for the forms by mail, you should ask for *any and all forms and materials available without charge for forming a new nonprofit corporation.* A sample letter is included as form 1 in Appendix C. However, for most states, it is easier to obtain the materials by phone or from the state's website.

You will need the information and forms for state tax exemption from your state Department of Revenue. The addresses, phone numbers, and websites are in

Appendix B. A form request letter is in Appendix C. For some states, you may be able to download the material from the Department of Revenue website. The state tax exemptions are explained in more detail in Appendix B.

If you plan to do charitable solicitation, in most states you will need to obtain information on any registration requirements from the state attorney general's office (in a few states it is a different office). The address, phone number, and basic requirements are listed in Appendix B. (More details on charitable solicitation laws are included in Chapter 6.)

IRS Forms and Instructions

The fastest way to get IRS forms is to download them from the Internet at **www.irs.gov**. However, because they are large booklets, it will tie up your line for a long time unless you have a fast connection. Another way to obtain them is to call the IRS forms office at 800-829-1040. (If this does not work in your area, check the federal government pages of your telephone book). The information you will need includes:

- ✪ Publication 557—*Tax Exempt Status for Your Organization*;

- ✪ Package 1023—*Application for Recognition of Exemption under Section 501(c)(3)*;

- ✪ Package 1024—*Application for Recognition of Exemption under sections other than Section 501(c)(3)*;

- ✪ Publication 526—*Charitable Contributions*;

- ✪ Publication 561—*Determining the Value of Donated Property*; and,

- ✪ Publication 598—*Tax on Unrelated Business Income*.

Define Your Purpose

Before forming your nonprofit organization, you should have a clear picture of your purpose and goals. You should then review the permissible purposes under the Internal Revenue Code and decide which type of organization you can be.

You will want to fit your purpose into the requirements for a Section 501(c)(3) organization if at all possible, so that people who contribute money to you can deduct it on their taxes.

If your activities fit into more than one area, you should stress the one that is permitted under Section 501(c)(3).

Example: If you are starting an organization because you are concerned about pesticides that cause cancer, you should not focus on the fact that you may want to lobby for laws against pesticides that cause cancer. If your primary function is to research pesticides or to educate the public as to which ones may be harmful, you could qualify as a Section 501(c)(3) organization that does scientific research or public education. If you later wanted to lobby, you could within your organization or you could form a separate organization to conduct substantial lobbying.

If the goal on your application is one that the IRS feels can only be achieved by legislation, they will deny your exemption as a Section 501(c)(3) organization. In such a case, you will either have form a noncharitable organization or redefine your goal.

Example: A goal such as abolishing nuclear weapons appears to be one that requires legislation. However, if educating the public on the dangers of nuclear proliferation is your goal, then depending on the programs you plan, you have a better chance to qualify as a charitable organization.

Review the IRS materials carefully and be sure that your purpose fits into one of the exempt categories. If you find this difficult or feel you may not be successful, you may want to consult with an attorney who specializes in nonprofit organizations. Since this application is one of the most important documents your organization will file, it will be worth the investment to get it right.

Choose and Search Your Name

While the activities and accomplishments of your organization will build up a reputation for its name, having a good name to begin with is a good way to appear more trustworthy. At the same time, the *wrong* kind of name (such as sounding like a commercial business) may raise questions with the IRS.

Choosing a Name

In choosing a name, you should use the following guidelines.

Use the right suffix. Some states require that certain words or suffixes be a part of the name of a company, such as "Inc." or "Assn." On the state sheets in Appendix B and on the materials from your state, you will find the rules that apply to the corporation's name.

Do not use forbidden words. Certain words, such as "olympic" or "trust," are not allowed to be a part of an organization's name under many states' laws. Most of these rules will be found either on the state sheets in Appendix B or on the materials from your state.

Do not be too similar. While there might seem to be some advantage to having your name sound like a similar group, such as the American Cancer Society or the American Red Cross, this leaves you open to a lawsuit by the other organization and possibly legal action by your state's attorney general. You can use a word such as cancer, heart, or diabetes if it relates to your organization's purpose, but do not intentionally make your name sound like another group's name.

Be sure it is not confusing. Many words in the English language are spelled differently from how they sound. Be sure that the name you choose is easy to spell so that people can locate your phone number or Web address easily.

Searching a Name

Once you have chosen the perfect name, you need to be sure that no one else has established legal rights to it. Many businesses have been forced to stop using their name after spending thousands of dollars in promotions because the name was already in use.

Legal rights can be established by registering a name as a trademark or by merely using the name. Consequently, you cannot be sure no one has rights to a name just by checking registered names. You need to check if anyone is using the name but has not yet registered it.

The following are places you should check.

Federal trademarks. First, you should check if anyone has registered the name as a federal trademark. This can be done on the Internet by going to the United States Patent and Trademark Office website (**www.uspto.gov**) and clicking the "Search" button under "Trademarks." If you do not have access to the Internet at home, you can use a computer in many libraries. If you are not familiar with how to access the Internet, a librarian may be able to perform the search for you for a small fee.

Yellow pages. You should search the Yellow page listings next. This can also be done online. Most sites check one state at a time, but **www.switchboard.com** can check all states. Since search engines are not always one hundred percent accurate, you should search on at least a few other sites for the state in which you will operate.

Web addresses. If you have any expectation of having a website some day, you should check if the Web address, or *uniform resource locator* (URL), is available. This can be done at **www.domainname.com.**

As a nonprofit organization, you will be able to use the designation ".org" (rather than ".com" or ".net"), but if you have a clever name you wish to use with ".com," you can use that. If the name you want is already taken in ".org," ".com," and ".net," it may be available in the new designations ".cc" and ".to." However, because the name is similar to an existing group, you run the risk of being sued and would be better off with a unique name.

Search services. If you are unable to access the Internet in any way or if you would rather have someone else do the search, you can hire a professional search firm. In addition to a trademark search, they can check other records around the country to give you a more accurate answer as to whether the name is being used anywhere. The cost can range from about $100 to over $800, depending on how thorough the search is and who is doing it. The following are a few firms that do searches. You can call or write to them for a quote.

Government Liaison Services, Inc.
200 N. Glebe Road, Suite 321
Arlington, VA 22203
GLS@Trademarkinfo.com
703-524-8200 or 800-624-6564
fax: 703-525-8451
www.trademarkinfo.com

Thomson & Thomson
500 Victory Road
North Quincy, MA 02171-3145
800-692-8833 or 617-479-1600
fax: 617-786-8273
www.thomson-thomson.com

Blumberg Excelsior Corporate Services, Inc.
4435 Old Winter Garden Road
P.O. Box 2122, Orlando, FL 32802
407-299-8220 or 800-327-9220
fax: 407-291-6912
www.blumberg.com.index2.html

Secretary of State. Finally, you should check with the Secretary of State in the state in which you will register your corporation to see if the name is available. In some states, this can be done over the phone or on the Internet. In others, you must send a written inquiry.

Registering the Name

After you have chosen the name for your new company and you have made sure that it is still available, you should register it before someone else does. You are allowed to reserve a name for a small fee in most states. However, it is usually better to send your **ARTICLES OF INCORPORATION** in as soon as you select a name. (see form 4, p.137)

By forming your corporation, you have ensured that no other person can register a company with the same name in your state. Nonetheless, this does not stop someone from registering the name with another state or from getting a federal trademark for it.

Trademarks

A federal trademark gives the owner the right to use the name anywhere in the United States and to stop most others from using it. But it does not eliminate the rights of those who have used the name previously.

Example: Suppose you form an Italian-American social club named Vesuvius Club, do a search, find no one using the same name, and register the name as a trademark. If you later learn that there is a group that has been using the name Vesuvius Club in San Francisco, but they do not have a trademark or telephone listing. You cannot stop them from using it in their area.

With a federal trademark, you can stop any new clubs from using the name, but not those who used it before you began.

With the Internet reaching into every corner of the world, there is an issue of Internet businesses infringing on the rights of small operators in remote locations. If you plan an operation with a significant Web presence, you may be sued by a small operator somewhere who has used the name before you. If you register a federal trademark and he or she has not, it would work in your favor, but there is now the open legal question of how thorough a business needs to be when doing a search.

One good way to see if anyone is using a name is to perform Web searches on the major search engines (Google, Yahoo, Excite, Altavista, Lycos) to see if your desired name is being used anywhere by anyone. If not, you are in good shape. If so, you need to determine if the other use conflicts with your intended use.

Before attempting to register your name, you should know the basics of federal trademarks.

- ✪ A *trademark* is technically the name of a mark applied to goods, while a *service mark* is a mark used with services. A nonprofit organization will usually provide services, so it will likely be registering a service mark.

- ✪ Trademarks and service marks are registered according to classes of goods or services. If you plan to use your mark in more than one class, you will need to register (and pay a filing fee of $335) for each class.

- ✪ Your trademark will not be granted until you have actually used the mark. You can file an application indicating your *intent to use* a mark, but you must actually use it before registration is official.

- ✪ In order to qualify for federal registration, you must use your mark *in commerce*, which means in a transaction with people in different states or with a foreign country. The use must be in *good faith*, meaning that you cannot just mail a copy to a relative.

- ✪ You can register your trademark with each state. This is not necessary if you plan to get a federal trademark immediately; but if you plan to limit your business to one state or do not plan to expand out of state for a number of years, state registration is faster and less expensive than federal registration.

You can get more information from the United States Patent and Trademark Office website at:

www.uspto.gov

Articles of Incorporation

To create a nonprofit corporation, a document must be filed with the state agency that keeps corporate records—usually the Secretary of State. In most states, this document is called the *articles of incorporation*; however, in some states, it may be called the *certificate of incorporation*, *articles of association*, or *charter*. For simplicity, this document is referred to as the **ARTICLES OF INCORPORATION** throughout this book.

Most states provide a blank form for the **ARTICLES OF INCORPORATION** and the IRS provides a sample of what they look for as **ARTICLES OF INCORPORATION**. Unfortunately, these two forms are in no way similar. What you will need to do in order to have articles that are acceptable to both your state and the IRS is to combine the requirements of both. This can be done in a few ways.

- ✪ A generic **ARTICLES OF INCORPORATION** form is included in this book. (see form 4, p.137) It contains the IRS requirements for Section 501(c)(3) organizations and the basic requirements of most states. Check your state material to see if there are any new or additional requirements, and if so, add these to Article 11 of form 4.

- ✪ Also included in this book is an **ADDENDUM TO ARTICLES OF INCORPORATION** form that includes the IRS requirements for Section 501(c)(3) organizations. (see form 5, p.139) You can use this form as an addendum to your state's form. This will not work for the states that do not provide blank articles of incorporation forms.

- ✪ You can take the requirements from your state's form and the IRS requirements from the addendum and retype them into a new **ARTICLES OF INCORPORATION** document.

If you are forming an organization that is exempt under a section other than Section 501(c)(3) (*e.g.* social welfare organizations under Section 501(c)(4) or social clubs under Section 501(c)(7)), you will need to use the third option above and retype the material applicable to your type of organization.

NOTE: *Some organizations have special requirements, for example, social clubs must be nondiscriminatory. For more information, see IRS Publication 557.*

If you are forming a private foundation (even though, as explained in Chapter 2, you should try to avoid it), you should obtain IRS Publication 578.

The following is a discussion of the articles included in the **ARTICLES OF INCORPORATION** form in this book. These articles are the common ones on most states' forms.

Article 1: Name of the corporation. Some states require nonprofit corporations to include a suffix like "Inc." or "Assn." at the end of their name, but others do not. Check the state pages in Appendix B for your state's requirements.

Article 2: Address of the corporation. The street address of the principal office, and if different, the mailing address of the corporation, should be provided.

Article 3: Purpose. The first sentence is the **required** language to qualify for Section 501(c)(3) status. After this, you must add the *specific* purpose of your organization. It is important to word this correctly or your exempt status may be denied by the IRS. Refer to IRS Publication 557 for guidance. If you have trouble drafting your purpose, consider consulting with a specialist in nonprofit law.

Article 4: Directors. Include the number of directors (most states require three but some allow just one) and their names and addresses.

Article 5: Private inurement and lobbying. This is required by the IRS to prevent the corporation from using its assets for private inurement and from lobbying the government. (see page 11.)

Article 6: Dissolution. This is required by the IRS so that if the corporation dissolves, the assets will go to another qualifying organization.

Article 7: The name of the registered agent and the address of the registered office, along with the agent's acceptance. Each corporation must have a registered agent (in some states called a statutory agent) and a registered office. The registered office can be the business office of the corporation if the registered agent works out of that office. It can be the office of another individual who is the registered agent (such as the corporation's attorney) or it can be a professional registered agent's office. In some states, it cannot be a residence unless the address is also a business office of the corporation.

> **Warning:** If you do not comply, you will be unable to maintain a lawsuit and you will possibly be fined.

Article 8: Members. In this section, check the box to designate whether or not the corporation will have members.

Article 9: Duration. In nearly all cases, you will want the duration of the corporation to be perpetual rather than for a set number of years.

Article 10: Name and address of the incorporator of the corporation. In some states this may be any person, even if that person has no future interest in the corporation. There are companies in state capitals that will have someone run over to the Secretary of State to file corporate articles that are later assigned to the real parties in interest.

Article 11: Additional requirements. Review the state pages in Appendix B and the materials from your state (or the state statute) to determine if any other matters are required to be included in the **ARTICLES OF INCORPORATION**. If so, include them here. If more than one matter needs to be included, like you can designate them Article 12, Article 13, etc.

Execution In most states, the **ARTICLES OF INCORPORATION** must be signed and dated by the incorporator in black ink. Typically, the registered agent must sign a statement accepting his or her duties as such. This can be done either as a separate form or on the same form as the **ARTICLES OF INCORPORATION**.

Filing The **ARTICLES OF INCORPORATION** form must be filed with the Secretary of State by sending it and the filing fees to the address listed in Appendix B. A duplicate copy must be included in most states. The fees (as available at time of publication) are listed in Appendix B as well. If you wish to receive a certified copy of the articles, which you will need for the nonprofit mailing permit, there is an additional cost.

NOTE: *It is possible in some states to file corporate papers by fax and to use a credit card for payment.*

The return time for the articles in most states is usually a week or two. If you need to have them back quickly, you might be able to send and have them returned by a courier such as FedEx, Airborne Express, or UPS, with prepaid return. Call your secretary of state for details.

Bylaws

Every corporation must have *bylaws*. This is the document that spells out in detail the corporation's purpose, its operating rules, and operational structure. For a nonprofit corporation, they are especially important and must be submitted to the IRS when applying for the tax exemption.

A generic set of **Bylaws** is included in this book. (see form 6, p.141) Read through this set carefully to be sure that everything in it will apply to your organization and that there is no conflict with your state laws. If you wish to make any major changes to them (such as powers, voting, or quorum), you should first check your state statutes to be sure that your provisions do not violate any section of the law.

As discussed in Chapter 2, it is not advisable to have formal members. If you decide to, you will need to add membership provisions to your **Bylaws**. These are included in the **Addendum to Bylaws**. (see form 7, p.147) Be sure to check the correct box in Article II of the **Bylaws** if you use this form.

Taxpayer Identification Number

Prior to opening a bank account, the corporation must obtain a taxpayer identification number (formally known as an employer identification number or EIN). This is the corporate equivalent of a Social Security number. You will need this number even if you do not expect to hire employees.

The number is obtained by filing **IRS Form SS-4**. (see form 8 p.149) This usually takes two or three weeks, so it should be filed early. Send the form to the Internal Revenue Service Center listed in the instructions.

If you need the identification number quickly, you can obtain it by calling the IRS phone number included in the instructions. Be sure to have your **IRS Form SS-4** completed and with you before calling.

When you apply for this number, you will probably be put on the mailing list for other corporate tax forms. If you do not receive these, call your local IRS office and request the forms for new businesses. These include Circular E (explains the taxes due), W-4 forms for each employee, the tax deposit coupons, and Form 941 (quarterly return for withholding).

Corporate Supplies

A corporation needs to keep a permanent record of its legal affairs. This includes the original state letter approving your organization, *minutes* of all meetings, lists of members, fictitious names registered, and any other legal matters. The records are usually kept in a ring binder. It is possible to purchase a specially prepared *corporate kit* that has the name of the corporation printed on it and usually contains forms such as minutes and bylaws. However, most of these items are included with this book, so purchasing such a kit might be unnecessary.

Some sources for corporate kits including the following.

Blumberg Excelsior
4435 Old Winter Garden Road
P.O. Box 2122, Orlando, FL 32802
407-299-8220
800-327-9220
Fax: 407-291-6912
www.blumberg.com/index2.html

Corpex
1440 Fifth Avenue
Bay Shore, NY 11706
800-221-8181
631-968-0277
Fax: 800-826-7739
631-968-0937
Email: Corpex@CorpexNet.com
www.corpexnet.com

CorpKit Legal Supplies
46 Taft Avenue
Islip, NY 11751-2112
888-888-9120
Fax: 888-777-4617
Email: info@corpkit.com
www.corpkit.com

Corporate Seal   One thing not included with this book is a *corporate seal*. This must be specially made for each corporation. Most corporations use a metal seal, like a notary's seal, to emboss the paper. This seal can be ordered from an office supply company. Some states now allow rubber stamps for corporate seals. Rubber stamps are cheaper, lighter, and easier to read. These can also be ordered from office supply stores, printers, and specialized rubber stamp companies. The corporate seal should contain the exact name of the corporation, the word "seal," and the year of incorporation.

Organizational Meeting

The real birth of the corporation takes place at the first meeting of the incorporators and the initial board of directors. The officers and board of directors are elected at this meeting. Other business also may take place, such as adopting employee benefit plans.

Usually, minutes, tax, and other forms are prepared beforehand and used as script for the meeting. They are read and voted on during the meeting and then signed at the end of the meeting.

Those items in the following agenda designated with boldface type are forms found in Appendix C of this book. These forms may be torn out of the book, photocopied, or rewritten as necessary to fit your situation.

Agenda   The agenda for the initial meeting is usually as follows.

1. Signing the **Waiver of Notice of Organizational Meeting**.

2. Noting persons present.

3. Presentation and acceptance of **Articles of Incorporation** (the copy returned by the secretary of state).

4. Election of directors.

5. Adoption of **Bylaws**.

6. Election of officers.

7. Presentation and acceptance of corporate seal.

8. Adoption of **BANKING RESOLUTION**.

9. Adoption of Resolution to Reimburse Expenses.

10. Adoption of any tax resolutions.

11. Adjournment.

Minute Book

After the organizational meeting, set up your *minute book*. The minute book usually contains the following.

✪ Title page ("Corporate Records of _____").

✪ Table of contents.

✪ The letter from the secretary of state acknowledging receipt and filing of the Articles of Incorporation.

✪ Copy of the Articles of Incorporation.

✪ Copy of any fictitious name registration.

✪ Copy of any trademark registration.

✪ Waiver of Notice of Organizational Meeting.

✪ Minutes of Organizational Meeting.

✪ Bylaws.

✪ Tax forms:

- IRS Form SS-4 and taxpayer identification number;

- IRS Forms 1023 or 1024; and,

- any state forms.

Bank Account

A corporation will need a bank account. Checks payable to a corporation cannot be cashed by an individual—they must be deposited into a corporate account. Fortunately, some banks have special rates for nonprofit organizations that are very reasonable.

All you should need to open a corporate bank account is a copy of your **ARTICLES OF INCORPORATION**, your taxpayer identification number, and perhaps a business license. Some banks, however, want more, and they sometimes do not even know what they want.

Example: After one individual opened numerous corporate accounts with only those items, he encountered a bank employee who wanted "something certified so we know who your officers are. Your attorney will know what to draw up." He explained that he was an attorney and the president, secretary, and treasurer of the corporation and would write out, sign, and seal whatever they wanted. The bank employee insisted that it had to be a nice certificate signed by the secretary of the corporation and sealed.

If you have trouble opening the account, you can use the **BANKING RESOLUTION** included with this book or you can make up a similar form. (see form 13, p.167)

Licenses

In some states, counties and municipalities are authorized to levy a license fee or tax on the *privilege* of doing business. Nonprofit corporations do not always come under these laws, but some areas have registration provisions to keep track of nonprofits. Check with your town, city, or county clerk to see if registration is required.

Charitable Solicitations
As explained in Chapter 6, if you will be doing charitable solicitations, many states will require you to register.

4 APPLYING FOR TAX EXEMPT STATUS

Although it is commonly thought that the Internal Revenue Service grants exemptions to nonprofit organizations, technically the IRS merely checks to see whether an organization is exempt. The exemption has already been granted by Congress. The IRS's only role is to recognize it.

Having your exemption recognized is an important and somewhat complicated process. You will need to read and understand the tax laws to correctly spell out a purpose for your organization that complies with the law.

If you know of any attorneys or accountants who offer low cost or free services to nonprofit organizations, you should consider using their services.

Charitable Organizations

As explained earlier, under the tax law, the word "charitable" does not only mean charities that help the poor—it means any organization that qualifies to receive tax deductible donations. If at all possible, you should structure your organization as a charitable organization under IRS Section 501(c)(3). If you cannot (for example, if you plan to do substantial lobbying or to participate in political campaigns), you will need to form a noncharitable organization under another section of the I.R.C. as explained in the next section.

Forms   If you sent for the materials mentioned in Chapter 3, you should have the forms and publications you will need. That material includes the following:

- ✪ Package 1023—Application for Recognition of Exemption;

- ✪ Form 8718—User Fee for Exempt Organization Determination Letter Request;

- ✪ Publication 557; and,

- ✪ Publication 578.

The *Application for Recognition of Exemption* (IRS Form 1023) is the form you need to file to be recognized as an exempt organization. Churches do not need to file the form. Organizations that receive less than $5,000 per year are not required to file, but they should file anyway for the benefits. Filing will:

- ✪ assure donors of deductibility of donations;

- ✪ allow exemption from state taxes;

- ✪ allow nonprofit postal rates; and,

- ✪ guaranty that the information from the form can be used later in other filings, such as state exemption applications or grant applications.

Considering the complexity of the law, the instructions and publications are fairly well written. They guide you through the form, line-by-line, and refer to other sections of the I.R.C. when necessary. If you are preparing your own application, be sure to read both the instructions to Form 1023 and Publication 557 thoroughly before beginning. The following are important issues to consider on the more difficult questions on Form 1023.

Part I. This part is fairly straightforward.

- ◈ For line 2, if you do not yet have your taxpayer identification number, you can include **IRS FORM SS-4** with this application.

- ◈ For line 10, you do not need to send a certified or file-stamped copy, but you do need to send a *confirmed copy.* A confirmed copy is one that agrees with the original. A photocopy of the original organizational document that is signed and dated will work. If it is unsigned, you need to attach a written declaration to the copies you send stating that they are "true and correct copies of the originals, which are on file with the Secretary of State."

Part II. This is the most important part, and question 1 is the most important question. You should read IRS Publication 557 and Chapter 5 of this book before attempting this. After reading these, if you feel that your answer may be questionable, you should check with an attorney or research some of the additional references in Appendix A.

◈   Line 2 is concerned with whether your organization is a public charity or private foundation. As explained in Chapter 2, it is important to be a public charity, so you must attempt to pass either the public support test or the facts and circumstances test.

◈   On line 4c you may want to have a public official on your board, but this is not necessary.

◈   Line 4d is about *disqualified persons*. These are the people who started, control, or are major contributors to the organization, and their family members. It is not a problem if these people are on the board or have relationships, but there will be a stricter scrutiny of the transactions to be sure there is not any excess benefit.

◈   If you check "yes" to any question on lines 5, 6, or 7, you should consult with an attorney to be sure the arrangement is allowable.

◈   For line 12a, it is okay if there are charges for the services (such as for museum entrance, copies of publications, etc.), but the basis of the fee should be to recover costs, not to make a profit.

◈   For line 12, it is better if the organization's benefits are available to the general public. If the benefits are limited to a certain group, that group must be a natural, reasonable limitation.

>   **Example:** Limiting an animal shelter to one county where there are existing groups operating in surrounding counties.

◈ You can admit to insubstantial lobbying on line 13 (as explained in Chapter 5); however, this just opens several new problems, and as a new organization, you should stay away from lobbying until you have a clear budget and can pass the tests.

◈ If you answer "yes" on line 14, your exemption will be denied.

Part III. This section answers technical requirements such as the effective date and whether the organization is a private foundation. Read Publication 557 and Chapter 5 again before answering these questions.

Part IV. Unless you are incorporating an existing association, you will need to prepare proposed budgets rather than financial statements. You may wonder how you can possibly know where your money will come from if you have just started, but you can at least make preliminary plans based on whether you will apply for grants or fund raise. It does not matter if your actual funding is different from your plans, as long as you are still able to pass the tests avoiding private foundation status.

While filling out the forms, keep in mind that, under the law, they will be public record and anyone can get a copy of them from the IRS or from you. (There is a penalty if you do not provide copies to those who request them.) Therefore, if there is any information that you need to include on the form but wish to keep private, such as donor lists or trade secrets, you can write "See Attachment" in the space for the information on the form. Then write on the attachment—"NOT SUBJECT TO PUBLIC INSPECTION"—and include the necessary information you wish to be concealed. Then you should attach a statement of why the information should be withheld from the public.

Noncharitable Organizations

If your organization cannot qualify as a charitable organization under Section 501(c)(3), you will need to apply under a different section of the code and use different IRS forms.

Following are some of the other types of nonprofit organizations that can apply for tax exemption and the code sections that they must qualify under.

Business leagues	Section 501(c)(6)
Chambers of commerce	Section 501(c)(6)
Civic leagues	Section 501(c)(4)
Employee associations	Section 501(c)(4), (9), or (17)
Labor organizations	Section 501(c)(5)
Lodges	Section 501(c)(10)
Recreational clubs	Section 501(c)(7)
Social clubs	Section 501(c)(7)
Social welfare organizations	Section 501(c)(4)
Veterans' organizations	Section 501(c)(19)

All of these organizations use Package 1024 (rather than 1023) to apply for recognition of tax exemption. The questions are similar to those discussed for charitable organizations, but the rules are not as strict. The main concern is that none of the directors or members receive any financial benefits from the organization.

NOTE: *If some of the directors or members receive salaries or rents from the organization, the rates must be reasonable and no higher than would be paid to a different person.*

Submitting Your Application

The forms should be filed within fifteen months after incorporation in order to have the tax exempt status apply from the corporation's beginning. If the forms are late, they only apply from the date of filing. However, you can get an extension if you ask before the the end of the fifteen months.

Along with your application, you will need to include **IRS FORM 8718**, *User Fee for Exempt Organization Determination Letter* (see form 9, p.157), financial statements for the previous three years (or proposed budgets for the next two), and copies of the corporation's **ARTICLES OF INCORPORATION** and **BYLAWS**. The copy of the articles must be *conformed*, meaning an exact copy. It is best to send a photocopy of the articles that has been date-stamped or certified by the secretary of state. Otherwise, you may need to include a written declaration certifying its authenticity. The copy of the **BYLAWS** need not be signed if it is submitted as an attachment to Form 1023.

Response to Your Application

The response from the IRS can be either yes, maybe, or no. If you have successfully completed the form to the satisfaction of the IRS, your exemption will be granted. If they are not sure your organization qualifies, they may ask for clarification or more information. If it appears that your group does not qualify, they will issue a *proposed adverse determination*. You have thirty days to appeal this ruling before it becomes final. For information of how to appeal, read IRS Publication 892, *Exempt Organization Appeal Procedures for Unagreed Issues.*

State Tax Exemptions

Most states also exempt many nonprofit organizations from income, property, sales, and other taxes. In most states, the exemption is automatic, either because the organization is formed as a nonprofit or the organization's exemption is recognized by the IRS.

You can find the addresses of the state Departments of Revenue and whether exemption is automatic or not in Appendix B. Also, you should write to the department and ask for the forms necessary for the state exemptions.

5

PROTECTING YOUR NONPROFIT STATUS

The rules are strict for nonprofit corporations. If they are broken, tax exempt status can be lost and you could owe additional taxes and penalties. This chapter explains the most important rules and how to avoid breaking them.

Private Inurement

The *private inurement doctrine* is one of the most important concepts of nonprofit law. It states that the funds and benefits of a nonprofit organization cannot go to any particular persons but must be used for the approved purpose of the organization. The rule keeps people from using the form of a nonprofit organization to avoid taxes for private transactions.

Example: If a wealthy individual wants to start a foundation to hire relatives instead of giving them taxable gifts or inheritance, that person cannot use the form of a nonprofit organization.

The rule does not make sense for organizations such as social clubs or trade associations, whose whole purpose is to give benefits to members rather than to society. For these organizations, the law contorts to say that the members can benefit from the organization, but only if all the members benefit, not just a few. Also, these groups are limited in how much of their funds can come from outside the group. Dues and contributions from members are not taxable, but if the group raises too much money from outsiders, that income may be taxable.

To help you understand what the private inurement doctrine requires, the following are some examples.

Example 1: A trade association can be formed by apple growers to promote the eating of apples, but it cannot only work to sell its members apples. It must promote the eating of apples in general.

Example 2: A social club can be set up for the benefit of an ethnic group, such as an Italian-Americans club. But it cannot give special benefits to some members, such as reduced dues, which are subsidized by other members.

Example 3: A scientific organization can be formed to test electrical products for safety, but it cannot work for the interests of just a few manufacturers.

Example 4: A museum can be set up to display and sell works of art, but not if its purpose is selling its members' works for their financial gain.

Excess Benefits Transactions

Besides not having the purpose be to benefit private parties, the actual operations of the group must not give excess profits to private individuals.

Nonprofit organizations are allowed to hire employees, rent property, and pay for services. In most cases, there is no prohibition against hiring, renting from, or buying from their own directors or officers—as long as it is a fair transaction. The salary must not exceed what is fair in the community, the rent must be fair market rent, and the services must not be overpriced compared to other providers of the same services.

Transactions between nonprofits and their directors, officers, and members will be looked at carefully by the IRS, so you should keep careful records and be able to back up all transactions.

Example: If a director rents office space to your organization, you should have evidence of how much rent is charged to others and what other rentals are available to the organization. If the organization pays salaries to employees and officers, you should document how much money those people have earned elsewhere and what similar organizations are paying similar employees.

Lobbying

A basic rule for charitable nonprofit corporations is that if a *substantial part* of the activities consist of *propaganda* or *attempting to influence legislation*, then the tax exemption will be denied or revoked.

Lobbying is considered to be either directly contacting legislators to influence legislation or attempting to influence public opinion on an issue of legislation. It is not considered lobbying to do a nonpartisan study or analysis or to respond to legislative requests for information.

What *substantial* means in the case of lobbying has been a contentious issue for a long time. Two tests exist that can be used by a nonprofit to be sure it does not violate the limit—the *substantial part test* and the *expenditures test*. All charities must pass the substantial part test, unless they elect to use the expenditures test. Churches and related organizations are not allowed to elect the expenditures test.

The expenditures test was devised because the substantial part test was difficult to understand and there were no strict standards to guide the IRS agents. According to the substantial part test, no more than fifteen percent of the organization's expenditures can be for lobbying. However, it is difficult to put a dollar value on many actions of an organization, so it is easy for an organization to err.

Example: How much money was expended if a group puts one paragraph in their newsletter promoting a legislative issue? Would you include a percentage of the printing, postage, and addressing, as well as the office rent and utilities?

Although the expenditures test was created to give organizations some certainty, few have used it because the IRS rules require much greater record keeping. According to the expenditures test, an organization is allowed to spend twenty percent of its first $500,000 on exempt purpose expenditures, fifteen percent of the next $500,000, ten percent of the next $1,000,000 and five percent of the rest. However, no group can spend more than $1,000,000 on lobbying. To pass the expenditures test, the organization must file IRS Form 5768 and must use Part VI-A of Schedule A, Form 990 to figure the limits.

Private Foundations

Private foundations under Section 501(c)(3) are not permitted to lobby at all.

Other Nonprofits

Nonprofit organizations that are exempt under provisions other than Section 501(c)(3), such as social welfare organizations and trade associations, do not need to limit lobbying. Thus, many charitable nonprofit organizations set up noncharitable nonprofit organizations to handle lobbying.

Penalty

The penalty for violating these rules can be a tax on the amounts expended or a complete loss of tax exempt status.

Further Information

The Nonprofit Lobbying Guide is a book that explains in detail the legislative process and how a nonprofit organization can lobby successfully and legally. It is available for $16 from Independent Sector (888-860-8118) or in PDF format for no charge at:

www.clpi.org/toc.html

Political Campaigning

Political campaigning is strictly controlled for nonprofits. Political campaigning is considered to be supporting of particular candidates for office (as opposed to lobbying, which is supporting legislation). The general rule is that charitable organizations may not do any political campaigning, while noncharitable nonprofits can only do limited campaigning. However, special organizations known as *political action committees* (PACs) can be set up to solely do political campaigning.

Like the rules against lobbying, these rules allow an organization to do nonpartisan voter information campaigns. For example, a group can send out pamphlets listing how legislators voted on particular issues, such as gun control and abortion, and not be considered as supporting any particular candidates. However, the pamphlets are supposed to be written in a nonpartisan manner, without indicating approval or disapproval of either record.

Although the tax law does not impose an absolute ban on political campaigning by nonprofits that are noncharitable, federal election laws severely limit what nonprofit corporations can do. For this reason, most nonprofit corporations that wish to participate in campaigns set up PACs for political campaigning.

Penalty   The penalty for violating these rules can be a tax on the amounts expended or a complete loss of tax exempt status.

Conflicts of Interest and Self-Dealing

It is not fatal for an organization to have dealings with its insiders (disqualified persons in IRS parlance), but the dealings require careful documentation and at times can look bad to outsiders. As previously discussed, any transactions with insiders should be documented.

Keep in mind that conflicts of interest and *nepotism* in an organization can have a negative effect on members or contributors. If the person who starts an organization only hires family members and no one else to work for the organization, this may be seen as a conflict of interest to those who make grants or want to join.

In some cases, the salaries in an organization are below normal and few other people are willing to get involved, so a conflict of interest may not occur. But in a large organization where many people want to be involved, these political problems may result in a loss of support or even in the formation of splinter groups.

> **Warning:** Avoid keeping any conflicts secret. If the organization is dealing with an insider or an insider's family member, do not try to hide it. Explain the person's relationship to the organization and put the transaction in the records.

Sources of Income

There are two main concerns for nonprofit organizations about the sources of income—new funds do not cause it to lose its public charity status and that not too much of the money is from sources unrelated to its exempt purpose.

Donations   As explained in Chapter 2, a charitable nonprofit organization does not want to be a private foundation. The only way to do this is to pass either the public support test or the facts and circumstances test. Mainly, it must be sure that the income comes from *public* sources rather than one or two donors. Keep these tests in mind when raising money, since this may mean declining certain donations if they threaten your public charity status.

Fundraising   Both charitable and noncharitable organizations must be careful about how they
Activities   earn money. If too much comes from improper sources, they may be required to pay tax penalties or completely lose their tax exemption. For charitable organizations, the basic rule is that the money-making activities must be related to the exempt function of the organization. For noncharitable organizations, only a limited amount may be raised from nonmembers.

Checklist for Avoiding Problems

- ☐ Dealings with insiders
    - ☐ Be sure the amount is reasonable
    - ☐ Keep detailed documentation
    - ☐ Do not hide deals
- ☐ Lobbying
    - ☐ Charitable organization—only insubstantial
    - ☐ Set up a separate organization if necessary
    - ☐ Noncharitable organizations—okay, but not deductible
- ☐ Political campaigning
    - ☐ No political campaigning
    - ☐ Only nonpartisan voter education
    - ☐ Set up a PAC for campaigning
- ☐ Sources of income
    - ☐ Watch public support limits
    - ☐ Limit unrelated income
    - ☐ Pay taxes on unrelated income

6 RAISING MONEY IN A NONPROFIT ORGANIZATION

A nonprofit organization cannot operate like a profit-making business—it is limited in the types of profit-making operations it may run. However, it has other possibilities for making money that are not open to profit-making companies.

Applying for Grants

A nonprofit corporation can qualify for grants from both private foundations and government agencies. There are thousands of grants available through various programs, some of which are not claimed by anyone. If you do some research, you may qualify for the fund you need to run your programs.

However, getting a grant is not always easy. If you do not answer the questions correctly or provide the required documentation, you will not get the grant. Writing grant applications has become a profession in itself—as a career, some people compile the information needed for organizations to qualify for grants.

As a new organization, you probably will not want to start using expensive grant-writing services. It will be a good educational experience for you to make some grant applications to learn the process. Grant applications are like tax returns, in that you can better use the services of a professional unless you have done it yourself and know what kind of information will be needed.

Fortunately, there are many organizations that help individuals and organizations learn how to apply for grants. One of the best is The Foundation Center. This organization compiles information about all of the foundations that give grants and makes it available in books, in libraries, and on their website. They have five centers—in Atlanta, Cleveland, New York, San Francisco, and Washington—and sponsor collections of foundation materials in two hundred libraries around the country. To locate their publications, check their website, **www.fdncenter.org**, or the largest library near you. Some of their publications include:

✪   *AIDS Fundraising*

✪   *Corporate Foundation Profiles*

✪   *The Foundation Directory*

✪   *Guide to U.S. Foundations, Their Trustees, Officers, and Donors*

✪   *National Directory of Corporate Giving*

✪   *National Guide to Funding in Arts and Culture*

✪   *National Guide to Funding for Community Development*

✪   *National Guide to Funding for the Environment and Animal Welfare*

✪   *National Guide to Funding in Health*

✪   *National Guide to Funding for Information Technology*

✪   *National Guide to Funding for Women and Girls*

For beginners, they have a grant tutorial that explains how to research and apply for grants. It can be found at:

http://fdncenter.org/learn/classroom

Soliciting Donations

For nonprofit organizations that cannot get grants or are intimidated by the application process, the primary way to gain funds is by soliciting donations from the public. For organizations that qualify under IRC Section 501(c)(3) as charitable, a donation is tax deductible for the giver. However, if a donor receives something for the donation, then only the amount in excess of the value of the item is deductible.

Example: If an organization holds a fundraising dinner at $100 a plate, and the value of the dinner is $25, then only $75 of the payment is tax deductible.

The IRS requires nonprofits to tell donors what portion of their payment is deductible.

Donations to other nonprofit organizations (social welfare, business leagues, etc.) are not deductible unless they are legitimate business expenses. Donations made to an organization (such as a trade association) that are normally deductible as business expenses are limited if the organization engages in lobbying. An organization that engages in lobbying must keep a record of what portion of its budget is used for lobbying and must let members know that this portion is not tax deductible.

Organizations should keep in mind that besides soliciting immediate gifts from the public, they should also look for bequests in peoples' wills. People who might only make small donations during their lifetime might be willing to make much greater contributions once they no longer need money. This is especially true of those with large estates and few or no children.

Charitable Solicitation Laws

Because of abuses by some nonprofits in the past, numerous laws regulate the solicitation of money for charitable purposes. Federal, state, and many local governments have acted to protect the public from abuses.

If you will be asking for donations from the public, you will need to comply with the laws or face civil or criminal penalties. In many states, your organization must register before it can begin solicitations. If you plan a national solicitation campaign, you will need to learn the laws of all fifty states.

Fortunately, there is a movement to simplify the process. A uniform registration form has been proposed and accepted by many states. Also, a great deal of guidance is available to nonprofits, much of it free.

Because of our constitutional guarantee of free speech, the regulation of fundraising by nonprofit organizations must be very narrowly drawn. Nonprofits are not considered commercial enterprises, so their regulation cannot be as broad as other areas. But the regulation that has been allowed is still a substantial burden and requires strict compliance.

Federal Laws   Federal laws concerned with charitable solicitations mostly deal with the tax aspects. The biggest abuse in this area occurs when donors are lead to believe that their payments to organizations are deductible when they are not.

Groups to which donations are not deductible are required to state in their solicitation that payments are not deductible as charitable contributions for federal income tax purposes. This rule does not apply to groups whose gross receipts are less than $100,000 a year, whose solicitation goes to less than ten people, or is only face-to-face. The penalty can be up to $10,000 if the violation is unintentional or fifty percent of the money collected if it is intentional.

Although donations to nonqualified groups are not deductible as charitable contributions, in some cases they may be deducted as business expenses.

Example: A real estate agent may deduct dues to a real estate board.

However, any part of the dues that is used to lobby the government is not deductible and organizations that are exempt under Sections 501(c)(4), (5), and (6) must make their members aware of what amount is not deductible.

For groups to which donations are deductible, there are three rules that must be followed when a donor gets something in exchange for their gift.

1. Only an amount in excess of the fair value of the premium is deductible.

2. When the amount is over $75, the donor must be given a written statement indicating what amount is deductible.

3. When a donation is over $250, the donor must be given a written receipt.

See IRS Publications 526 and 557.

State Laws
The biggest burden on fundraising by nonprofits is that most states require registration and disclosure. Some also require filing fees or bonds that can cost hundreds of dollars. For national organizations, it is a considerable burden to keep track of the laws in all fifty states, send for the filing forms, keep track of all the different deadlines, and compile all the required information. For small nonprofits just starting out, it is practically impossible.

If you are a new organization that needs to raise funds, follow these guidelines. First, find out if you are exempt. Each state has different categories of groups that are exempt. Exempt groups typically include religious organizations, schools, hospitals, and some clubs. Also, most states have a dollar limit, such as $10,000 or $25,000, and you are exempt until your donations reach that level. The dollar limits for each state are included in Appendix B. However, since the laws often change, check to be sure the figures are current. One good place to find information on state requirements is the following website:

www.raffa.com

If you do not fit under any of these exemptions, you will need to consider registration. If you will be doing most of your fundraising in your own state, you should start by getting the registration information (if registration is required in your state) and by learning the system so you can comply with those regulations. Next, you could expand your fundraising into the states that do not have registration requirements. These are:

✪   Delaware

✪   Hawaii

✪   Idaho

✪   Indiana

✪ Iowa

✪ Montana

✪ Nevada

✪ South Dakota (telephone solicitors must register)

✪ Texas

✪ Vermont

✪ Wyoming

Your next step could be to start registering on a state-by-state basis. If your potential donors are concentrated in a few states, then of course, those are the best ones to start with. If not, you could start with the states with the simplest or cheapest registration or the states with the highest population.

Just as there is a big difference in what each state requires, there is a difference in how seriously each state keeps track of registrations. Some states demand strict compliance and have teams of attorneys investigating nonprofit compliance, while others just pile the registration forms in a warehouse. If you find that strict compliance is not possible because of your group's limited resources, here are some things to consider.

Mail Solicitations. The United States Supreme Court has ruled that states do not have the right to require companies to collect sales taxes if they do not do business in that state. Mailing catalogs to and placing advertisements in a state is not considered doing business. Some have argued that merely mailing charitable solicitations to people in a state is not enough to require registration in that state, but there has not yet been a definitive court ruling on this.

Your group could take the position that sending a few solicitations by mail to a state is not enough to require your registration. Most likely, your letters will not be brought to the attention of the regulators anyway. However, if they do find out about it and decide that you should have registered, you may have to pay legal fees to resolve the matter. If your promotional materials are honest and you use the funds legitimately, you will be in much better position than if your materials are misleading or your promotion a scam.

Internet Solicitations. The Internet has added new legal issues to the matter of charitable solicitations. A few courts have ruled that anyone who has a website is legally *doing business* every place that can view the site. This has lead to some conclusions that might seem ridiculous, since a New York website owner can be guilty of violating a German obscenity law, for example.

If this rationale is accepted, the strictest law of any town on the planet controls every site on the Internet. Therefore, states that insist that anyone with a website comes under its jurisdiction are most likely wrong and soliciting funds on your website should not bring you under the jurisdiction of all fifty states. However, keep in mind that the law is not yet clear on this point and some states insist that all websites are under its jurisdiction.

If you are registered in some states and not others, you could put a disclaimer on your website that it is only intended for residents of those states. This should protect you, but as the law is new and still in flux, no one can be sure in every case.

Uniform Registration Statement. Because the different registration requirements of the different states create such a burden on interstate nonprofit organizations, many states have attempted to standardize the process. Instead of a different form with different requirements for each state, they have proposed a *Uniform Registration Statement* (URS) that could be used for all states.

Not all states have agreed to this since it has to go through hearings in each state legislature. But many states have, and in time, there may be just one form for all states.

At the time of this publication the following states and districts have agreed to accept the URS.

✪ Alabama	✪ Massachusetts	✪ Ohio
✪ Arkansas	✪ Michigan	✪ Oklahoma
✪ California	✪ Minnesota	✪ Oregon
✪ Connecticut	✪ Mississippi	✪ Pennsylvania
✪ District of Columbia	✪ Missouri	✪ Rhode Island
✪ Georgia	✪ Nebraska	✪ South Carolina
✪ Illinois	✪ New Hampshire	✪ Tennessee
✪ Kansas	✪ New Jersey	✪ Utah
✪ Kentucky	✪ New Mexico	✪ Virginia
✪ Louisiana	✪ New York	✪ Washington
✪ Maine	✪ North Carolina	✪ West Virginia
✪ Maryland	✪ North Dakota	✪ Wisconsin

In addition to the URS, Arkansas, Georgia, Mississippi, North Dakota, Tennessee, and West Virginia require supplemental forms. An excellent source of information on the state requirements can be found at:

www.multistatefiling.org

The following states require registration but do not accept the URS: Arizona, Colorado, and Florida. The following states do not require registration: Idaho, Indiana, Iowa, Montana, Nevada, South Dakota, Texas, Vermont, and Wyoming.

Local Laws Besides the state laws, numerous cities and towns have their own charitable solicitation laws. While many of these only apply to in-person, door-to-door, or telephone solicitors, some expect every group conducting a national campaign to register.

If you are conducting a local fundraising campaign, check with the clerk of any city or town in which you will be operating. Checking with every town in the nation is clearly beyond the ability of most new groups. When you grow, you may need to hire a professional fundraiser who can keep track of such compliance.

Constitutional Issues Regulating charitable solicitations raises some serious constitutional issues, most importantly, free speech. While states have argued that soliciting money is a commercial activity that is subject to regulation, the United States Supreme Court has held that asking for money for charitable causes is *not* commercial speech but is a highly protected form of free speech.

Whereas most laws only need to be reasonable to be valid, any laws that regulate charitable fundraising must be as limited as possible to achieve only a legitimate and narrow governmental interest. The government cannot use broad formulas, such as percentages of net proceeds that go to charity, to limit solicitations, and they cannot require lengthy disclosures to be made during verbal solicitations.

If you feel that a regulation violates your constitutional rights, you can ignore it. However, keep in mind that if someone complains and if you are investigated and charged with violating the law, you will need to take the time and money to defend yourself or face the penalties.

States have been able to regulate trespassing, gambling, fraud, and disclosure. Laws on these subjects that affect charitable solicitors will usually be upheld.

Unrelated Business Income

To keep nonprofit organizations from competing unfairly with profit-making businesses, there are strict limits on how much unrelated income such groups can have. Violation of the limits can result in tax penalties or loss of tax-exempt status. In all cases, unrelated business income is taxed and a separate tax form must be filed for the taxable income.

There are some exemptions for nonprofits that allow income to be raised without penalty. An organization cannot regularly operate an unrelated trade or business. But if an organization operates a business only sporadically, such as hosting an annual fund drive, the income is exempt. Also, if the business is related to its exempt function, such as a cafeteria in a hospital or a bookstore in a school, then the business is exempt.

Exempt Activities Besides the exemptions explained above for related and sporadic income sources, nonprofit organizations can earn some exempt types of income without penalty. These include:

- activities carried on primarily for the benefit of the members, employees, patients, students, or officers of the organization;

- activities done by volunteers, such as a car wash, carnival, or Christmas tree sale;

- renting out the organization's list of donors;

- selling items donated to the organization, such as a baked goods, books, or clothing;

- low cost items given for donations, such as address labels, Christmas seals, or greeting cards;

- trade shows about the organization's exempt function;

- interest, dividends, and royalties;

- rents; and,

- profits on sale of property owned by the organization.

Associate Members

In recent years, the IRS has penalized organizations that have different classes of members. Typically, a tax exempt group will have regular members and associate members who do not usually participate in the group in the same manner as regular members, but who get many of the same benefits. Currently the IRS says that if the rights and participation between different classes of members are too different, then the associates' member dues are unrelated business taxable income. (For guidance, see IRS Revenue Procedure 95-21.)

Affinity Programs

Nonprofits can also earn extra income by endorsing certain products, such as car rental companies or long distance carriers, to its members and can earn a percentage of the income generated. Some groups sponsor their own credit cards, with the symbols of their organization appearing on the card.

Such arrangements can either be unrelated business taxable income or exempt royalty income, depending on how the deal is structured. If it is a passive arrangement in which the group receives a royalty for use of its logo, the income is nontaxable. If the members of the group must materially participate, such as by promoting the products, the income is then taxable. (For guidance, see IRS Revenue Ruling 81-178 (1981-2 C.B. 135).)

Corporate Sponsorship

Income received from corporations for sponsoring events run by nonprofit corporations may or may not be taxable, depending on whether the corporate sponsor is *promoted* or merely *identified* at the event. Displaying a brand, logo, or name of a sponsor; listing products or services; or, giving addresses or phone numbers is considered identification. But promoting products, giving prices or discounts, and suggesting people buy the products are considered promotions and any money received for them is taxable. (For guidance, see IRS Proposed Regulation 1.513-4.)

7

RUNNING A NONPROFIT ORGANIZATION

Because of the stringent rules for nonprofits, they must be much more careful in following the correct procedures in their day-to-day operations. This chapter explains the important rules.

Day-to-Day Activities

On a day-to-day basis, there are not many differences between running a non-profit corporation and any other type of business or corporation. Most importantly, you must remember the prohibitions explained in Chapter 1. Make sure that everyone in the organization is aware of these.

The prohibition on mixing personal and business matters in a for-profit corporation is even stronger in a nonprofit. Do not write corporation checks for your personal expenses, even if you pay them back quickly. Do not do favors for relatives with corporation assets. Treat the corporation as if you are responsible for taking care of it for someone else.

Another important thing to remember is to *always* refer to the corporation as a corporation. *Always* use the complete corporate name including designations such as "Inc." or "Assn." *Always* sign corporate documents with your corporate title.

> **Warning:** If you do not use the complete corporate name and your title, you may lose your protection from liability. Several times people have forgotten to put the word "president" after their name when entering into contracts for the corporation. As a result, they were determined to be personally liable for the contract.

As explained in Chapter 1, you should obtain a copy of your state's nonprofit corporation laws and become familiar with them. Some states have specific requirements that must be complied with and you are expected to know what is required of your organization.

Corporate Records

The laws that records must be kept on are slightly different in each state. You should review your state statute and make a list of which records are required and then keep those records together with the list. The following are some typical rules.

Articles and Bylaws   Copies of the **ARTICLES OF INCORPORATION**, **BYLAWS**, and any revisions of these must be kept on hand by the corporation.

Minutes   A corporation must keep **MINUTES** of the proceedings of its board of directors, its members (if any), and any committees. The **MINUTES** should be in writing. Some states allow **MINUTES** to be kept in forms other than writing, provided they can be converted into written form within a reasonable time, so they can be kept in a computer or even on a videotape. However, it is always best to keep a duplicate copy or at least one written copy. Accidents can easily erase magnetic media. Blank forms that can be used for **MINUTES** are included in Appendix C. (see form 11, p.161)

Finances   A nonprofit corporation must keep accurate financial records, especially if it is engaged in charitable solicitations. These records usually include records of all receipts and disbursements as well as tax returns and any other financial reports that are filed.

Members   If the corporation has members, it must usually keep accurate records of the names and addresses of the members. Some states require the records to be in alphabetical order.

Meetings

The corporation must hold an annual meeting of the board of directors. If there are formal members, they must have a meeting as well. Usually, the members elect directors and the directors, in turn, elect officers. Minutes of these meetings must be kept with the corporate records. Forms for the **MINUTES OF ANNUAL MEETING OF DIRECTORS** are included in Appendix C. (see form 15, p.171) You can use these forms as master copies to photocopy each year. All you need to change is the date, unless the officers or directors change, or you need to take some other corporate action.

Annual Reports

Most states require that each corporation file an annual report. Some states require only one report every two years. Fortunately, the report is a simple, often one-page, form that is sent to the corporation by the secretary of state and may simply need to be signed and dated. It contains the taxpayer identification number, officers' and directors' names and addresses, the registered agent's name, and the address of the registered office. It must be signed and returned with the required fee by the date specified. If it is not, the corporation is dissolved after notice is given.

Charitable Solicitation Most states that require registration for charitable solicitation also require annual reports and some require detailed financial reports. The state pages in Appendix B tell whether an annual report is required and provide the address you can write to for more information.

Tax Returns

Federal Most nonprofit corporations are required to file a Form 990 tax return each year. If the income is below $100,000 and assets below $250,000, then Form 990EZ can be filed. If the income is less than $25,000 or the corporation is a church, school, or related organization, it may be exempt from filing. Check the instructions for the latest Form 990 to see if you qualify as exempt.

If your organization is a private foundation or has unrelated business income, you may need to file Form 990-PF or 990-T. If a charitable organization makes a political contribution of over $100, it must file Form 1120-POL. Check the instructions for these forms or Publication 598 if these situations apply to you.

In some cases, nonprofit corporations must file *interim tax returns.* If a charitable nonprofit organization receives a donation of certain types of property and sells or disposes of it within two years, the organization must file Form 8282 with the IRS and give a copy to the donor. Also, Form 8300 must be filed if more than $10,000 in cash is received.

All organizations that have employees must make regular deposits of taxes withheld (quarterly or more, often depending on the amount) and Form 941 must be filed quarterly reporting these deposits.

State   Some states require annual filings by nonprofits, some waive them once they are exempt, and others just want copies of the federal return. The addresses and phone numbers of state revenue offices are listed in Appendix B.

Employment Requirements

If you will be paying wages to anyone, even yourself, you will need to comply with all of the employer reporting and withholding laws of both your state and the federal government. The following is a summary of most of the requirements.

New hire reporting. To improve the enforcement of child support payments, all employers must report the hiring of each new employee to an agency in the state.

Employment eligibility. To combat the hiring of illegal immigrants, employers must complete the Department of Justice Form I-9 for each employee.

Federal tax withholding. Social security and income taxes must be withheld from employees' wages and deposited to an authorized bank quarterly, monthly, or more often, depending on the amount. The initial step is to obtain a Form W-4 from each employee upon hiring. (This same form can also be used to fulfill the new hire reporting law discussed above.)

State withholding. In states that have income taxes, there is usually a withholding and reporting requirement similar to the federal one.

Local withholding. In cities that have income taxes, there is usually a withholding and reporting requirement similar to the federal one.

Unemployment compensation. Employers must pay taxes on employee wages to the state and federal governments regularly. Also, employers must submit reports both quarterly and annually.

Workers' compensation. Depending on the number of employees and the type of work, the state may require that the employer obtain workers' compensation insurance.

Training

Many training programs and manuals are available to nonprofit organizations, so if you, your board of directors, or your officers are unfamiliar with nonprofits, consider this training. Many of the resources listed in Appendix A sponsor programs, publish manuals, and have educational websites. Because the rules for nonprofits are different from those of for-profit businesses, you should encourage everyone in your group to learn as much as possible.

GLOSSARY

A

annual report. A document filed by a corporation or limited liability company each year that usually lists the officers, directors, and registered agent.

articles of incorporation. The document that demonstrates the organization of a corporation.

articles of organization. The document that demonstrates the organization of a limited liability company.

association. A group of individuals united but not incorporated for a purpose.

B

blue sky laws. Laws governing the sales of securities.

bylaws. Rules governing the conduct and affairs of a corporation.

C

C corporation. A corporation that pays taxes on its profits.

certificate of incorporation. *See articles of incorporation.*

charitable. Qualifying under the tax laws to allow donors to deduct donations.

common stock. The basic ownership shares of a corporation.

contract. An agreement between two or more parties.

corporation. An organization recognized as a person in the law that is set up to conduct a business that shareholders own and officers and directors run.

D

distributions. Money paid out to owners of a corporation or limited liability company.

E

employee. Person who works under another person's control and direction.

employer identification number. Number issued by the Internal Revenue Service to identify taxpayers who do not have social security numbers.

estate planning. Preparing such documents as a will, trust, and other arrangements to control the passing of one's property at death.

exemption. The ability to sell certain limited types of securities without full compliance with securities registration laws.

F

fictitious name. The name a business uses that is not its personal or legal name.

G

general partnership. A business that is owned by two or more persons.

grant. Money given away to attempt to accomplish a purpose.

I

intangible property. Personal property that does not have physical presence, such as ownership interest in a corporation.

intellectual property. Legal rights to the products of the mind, such as writings, musical compositions, formulas, and designs.

L

liability. The legal responsibility to pay for an injury.

limited liability company. An entity recognized as a legal "person" that is set up to conduct a business owned and run by members.

limited liability partnership. An entity recognized as a legal "person" that is set up to conduct a business owned and run by professionals, such as attorneys or doctors and taxed as a partnership.

limited partnership. A business that is owned by two or more persons, of which one or more is liable for the debts of the business and one or more has no liability for the debts.

lobbying. Attempting to influence government actions.

M

membership agreement. A contract controlling the operation of a limited liability company in which the company is run by members.

management agreement. A contract controlling the operation of a limited liability company in which the company is run by its managers.

minutes. Records of the proceedings of corporate meetings.

N

nonprofit corporation. An entity recognized as a legal "person" that is set up to run an operation in which none of the profits are distributed to controlling members.

O

occupational license. A government-issued permit to transact business.

operating agreement. A contract among members of a limited liability company spelling out how the company will be run.

option. The right to buy stock at a future date, usually at a predetermined price.

organizational meeting. The meeting of the founders of a corporation or limited liability company during which the company is structured and prepared to begin business.

P

par value. A value given to newly-issued stock. This used to have legal significance, but now usually does not relate to anything except taxation in some states.

partnership. A business formed by two or more persons.

personal property. Any type of property other than land and the structures attached to it.

piercing the corporate veil. When a court ignores the structure of a corporation and holds its owners responsible for its debts or liabilities.

political action committee (PAC). An organization formed to aid political campaigns.

private foundation. A nonprofit organization that does not qualify as a public charity.

private inurement. Benefiting a private person rather than the public.

professional association. An entity recognized as a legal "person" that is set up to conduct a business of professionals, such as attorneys or doctors and taxed as a corporation.

promoters. Persons who start a business venture and usually offer interests for sale to investors.

proprietorship. A business that is owned by one person.

R

registered agent. The person authorized to accept legal papers for a corporation or limited liability company, sometimes called a *resident agent*.

resident agent. *See registered agent.*

S

S corporation. A corporation in which profits are taxed to shareholders.

Section 501(c)(3) organization. An organization that has been granted tax exempt status under Section 501(c)(3) of the Internal Revenue Code.

securities. Interests in a business such as stocks or bonds.

shareholder agreement. A contract among the owners of a corporation that spells out their rights.

shares. Units of stock in a corporation.

stock. Ownership interests in a corporation.

T

tangible property. Physical personal property such as desks and tables.

tax deductible. Contributions that donors can deduct from their taxable income.

tax exempt. Money received on which no tax needs be paid.

trademark. A name or symbol used to identify the source of goods or services.

transferability. The ability to sell shares of stock in a corporation.

trust. Arrangement in which property is held and used for a specific purpose.

U

usury. Charging an interest rate higher than that allowed by law.

W

withholding. Money taken out of an employee's salary for the government.

Z

zoning. Governmental regulation controlling the use of real property.

APPENDIX A: RESOURCES FOR NONPROFIT ORGANIZATIONS

This appendix includes organizations, websites, and books that offer useful information to nonprofit organizations.

Organizations

Alliance of Nonprofit Mailers
1211 Connecticut Ave NW #620
Washington, DC 20036-2701
202-462-5132
www.nonprofitmailers.org

Accounting Aid Society
18145 South Mack Avenue
Detroit, MI 484224-1444
313-647-9620
www.accountingaidsociety.org

Aspen Washington D.C.
One Dupont Circle, NW #700
Washington, DC 20036-1133
202-736-5800
www.aspeninst.org

Boardsource
1828 L Street, NW #900
Washington, DC 20036-5114
800-883-6262
www.boardsource.org

The Foundation Center
79 Fifth Avenue
New York, NY 10003
212-620-4230
www.fdncenter.org

**National Council of
Nonprofit Associations**
1030 15th St. NW Suite 870
Washington, DC 20005
202-962-0322
www.ncna.org

Websites

Center for Excellence in Nonprofits
   www.cen.org
Compass Point Nonprofit Services
   www.compasspoint.org
Council on Foundations
   www.cof.org
Don Kramer's Nonprofit Issues *(online newsletter)*
   www.nonprofitissues.com
Internal Revenue Service
   www.irs.ustreas.gov/charities/index.html
Internet Nonprofit Center
   www.nonprofits.org
The Nonprofit Resource Center
   www.not-for-profit.org
Thompson & Thompson, P.C. *(nonprofit tax issues)*
   www.taxexemptlaw.com
University of Wisconsin - Madison *(resources for starting a nonprofit)*
   www.library.wisc.edu/libraries/Memorial/grants/npweb.htm

Books

The following books provide detailed information on all aspects of nonprofit organization law. If you have a specific question, you may find the answer in these. However, some of them cost over a hundred dollars, so you might want to review them at a law library if you are new and on a limited budget.

The Legal Answer Book for Nonprofit Organizations, Hopkins, Bruce R., Wiley, John, & Sons, Inc., 1996

Nonprofit Corporations, Organizations & Associations, Oleck, Howard L. and Stewart, Martha E., Prentice Hall

Nonprofit Enterprises: Law and Taxation, Phelan, Marilyn E., Callaghan

Nonprofit Law Dictionary, Hopkins, Bruce R., Wiley, John, & Sons, Inc.

Parliamentary Law and Practice for Nonprofit Organizations, Oleck, Howard L. & Green, Cami, ALI-ABA, 1994

The Second Legal Answer Book for Nonprofit Organizations, Hopkins, Bruce R., Wiley, John, & Sons, Inc., 1999

The following books are available from The Foundation Center:

The 21st Century Nonprofit

America's Nonprofit Sector: A Primer

The Board Member's Book

Best Practices of Effective Nonprofit Organizations

The Handbook on Private Foundations

The Nonprofit Entrepreneur

Promoting Issues and Ideas

APPENDIX B: STATE-BY-STATE NONPROFIT LAWS AND ADDRESSES

The following pages contain a listing of each state's nonprofit corporation laws and fees. Because the laws are constantly being changed by state legislatures, you should call before filing your papers to confirm the fees and other requirements. The phone numbers are provided for each state.

In the continued growth of the World Wide Web, more and more state corporation divisions are making their fees and procedures available online. Some states have downloadable forms available and some even allow you to search their entire database from the comfort of your home or office.

The best websites at the time of publication of this book are included for each state. However, the sites change constantly, so you may need to look a little deeper if your state's site has changed its address.

• • • • •

Acknowledgement

Special thanks must be given to my wife Alexandra Schiller Warda, who helped me completely update this appendix.

Alabama

INCORPORATION:

Secretary of State
Corporations
P.O. Box 5616
Montgomery, AL 36103-5616
334-242-5324
www.sos.state.al.us/business/corpdl.cfm

What they supply:

State provides two copies of fill-in-the-blanks Articles of Incorporation. You can download the form from the Internet. The Adobe® Acrobat Reader™ is required for a successful download.

What must be filed:

You need to file the original and two copies of the Articles of Corporation in the county where the corporation's registered office is located.

Name requirements:

The corporate name shall not be the same as, or deceptively similar to, the name of any other corporation existing in Alabama. The name may not contain a word or phrase that indicates it is organized for a purpose other than contained in the Articles of Incorporation.

Directors requirements:

Your corporation must be have at least three directors. You have to fix the number of directors by the bylaws. The directors may be divided in classes and the terms of the different classes need not to be uniform.

Articles requirements:

*   the name of the corporation
*   the period of duration
*   the purpose of the corporation
*   any provisions for the regulation of the internal affairs (including final liquidation)
*   local and mailing address
*   number of the directors constituting the initial board of directors and names and addresses of the initial directors.
*   name and address of each incorporator

Filing fees:

The Judge of Probate filing fee is $25 and the Secretary of State's fee is $20. Both fees are payable to the Judge of Probate.

Reports:

You have to file an annual report between January 1 and March 15.

Statute: Alabama Code 10-3A-1 to 225

TAXES:

Alabama Department of Revenue
Corporate Section
50 N. Ripley Street
Montgomery, AL 36132-7123
334-242-1170
www.ador.state.al.us

Automatic exemption: No

CHARITABLE SOLICITATION:

Office of Attorney General
Consumer Protection Section
11 S. Union Street
Montgomery, AL 36130
205-242-7334

Statute: Alabama Code 13A-9-70, *et seq.*

Exemption:

Less than $25,000, provided that all fundraising functions are carried out by volunteers.

Annual filing: Yes

Accept URS: Yes

Alaska

INCORPORATION:

Dept. of Community and Economic Development
Division of Banking, Securities and Corporations
Corporation Section
P.O. Box 110808
Juneau, AK 99811-0808
907-465-2530
Fax: 907-465-5442
www.dced.state.ak.us/bsc/corps.htm

What they supply:

State sends material within two weeks. State provides fill-in-the-blanks Articles of Incorporation with sample Bylaws.

What must be filed:

Print or type your documents in dark, legible print and file two copies of the Articles of Incorporation. Computer print must be high resolution, laser print quality, suitable for microfilming. Make sure your documents bear the original signatures and are both notarized. Enclose the filing fee. One copy will be returned to you for your records. Paper must be no larger than 8 by 11 inches.

Name requirements:

The corporate name may not contain a word or phrase that indicates or implies that it is organized for a purpose other than one or more of the purposes contained in your Articles of Incorporation.

Directors requirements:

Your nonprofit corporation must have at least three initial directors. The number of directors has to be fixed by the Bylaws later on but the initial board of directors shall be fixed by the Articles of Incorporation.

The directors do not have to be residents of Alaska or members of the corporation, unless the Articles or Bylaws require so. The director's default term is one year.

Articles requirements:

You must state the names, telephone numbers, and addresses of your initial (first) board of directors in Article 6. In Alaska there must be at least three incorporators who must be natural persons at least 19 years old. Enter the names and (business) addresses of these incorporators in Article 7. Make sure that your Articles are notarized. The Articles should contain a statement that they are being filed under the provisions of the *Alaska Nonprofit Corporation Act* (AS 10.20).

Include in the Articles the following:

- the name of the corporation
- the period of duration, which may be perpetual
- the purpose or purposes for which the corporation is organized
- any provisions for the regulation of the internal affairs (including final liquidation)
- physical address of its initial registered office and the name of its initial registered agent
- number of the directors constituting the initial board of directors and names and addresses of persons who are to serve as the initial directors
- the name and address of each incorporator

Filing fees:

$50, payable to the State of Alaska Department of Commerce and Economic Development.

Reports: You have to file an annual report by July 2.

Statute: Alaska Statutes, Section 10.06.208-210

TAXES:

Alaska Department of Revenue
333 W. Willoughby Ave.
P.O. Box 110420
Juneau, AK 99811-0420
907-465-2322
Fax: 907-465-2375
www.revenue.state.ak.us

Automatic Exemption: Yes

CHARITABLE SOLICITATION:

Department of Law - Civil Division
Fair Business Practices Section
1031 W 4th Avenue, Ste 200
Anchorage, AK 99501-1994
907-269-5100

Statute: Alaska Statutes, Title 45, Chapter 68

Exemption: First $5.000 or 10 or less donors

Annual filing: Yes

Accept URS: No

Arizona

INCORPORATION:

Corporations Division
Arizona Corporation Commission
1300 W. Washington
Phoenix, AZ 85007-2929

Corporate Records Section:
602-542-3026
800-345-5819 (In-State only)
Fax: 602-542-0082

Corporate Filing Section:
602-542-3135
Fax: 602-542-4990

Tucson Office
Tucson Corporations Division
400 W. Congress
Tucson, AZ 85701-1347
520-628-6560
Fax: 520-628-6614
www.cc.state.az.us/corp/filings/forms/index.htm

What they supply:

State sends material within two weeks. State provides fill-in-the-blanks sets of Articles of Incorporation, both for corporations that propose tax exempt status and also for corporations that will be subject to taxation. They also provide a Certificate of Disclosure and a sample cover letter for filing your Articles.

What must be filed:

Complete your Articles and file the original and two copies. Also fill in the Certificate of Disclosure and attach it to your Articles. Enclose the filing fee. After filing your Articles must be published within 60 days in a newspaper of general circulation in the county of the place of business in Arizona. There must be three consecutive publications of a copy of the approved Articles. Within 90 days of filing an affidavit evidencing the publication must be filed with the Commission.

Name requirements:

Check your corporate name with the Commission prior to filing your documents by calling 602-542-3026 in Phoenix or 520-628-6560 in Tucson or on the website:
www.cc.state.az.us/corp/filings/namesearch.htm

A name may be formally reserved for a $10 fee for 120 days.

Directors requirements:

Your corporation must have one director. The names and addresses of the initial directors must be entered in Article 9.

Articles requirements:

Enter one of the specific valid purposes for which a nonprofit corporation may be formed in Article 3.

In Article 5 and 6 you must enter the applicable Section number of of the IRS code under which your corporation plans to organize. Contact your local IRS office to obtain these numbers.

In Article 8 enter the name and business address of your initial statutory agent. This statutory agent has to sign the Articles on the bottom of the page.

Also complete your Certificate of Disclosure that has to be filed with your Articles. It contains information about your officers, directors, and anyone involved in the corporation.

Filing fees:

$40, payable to the Arizona Corporation Commission. For expedited service, add an extra $35.

Reports:

The annual report must be filed by April 15 (or by the 15th day of the 4th month of the corporation's fiscal year if a different fiscal year, has been adopted).

Statute: Arizona Revised Statutes, Section 10-2300

TAXES:

Department of Revenue
Corporate Section
P.O. Box 29079
Phoenix, AZ 85038-9079
800-352-4090
Fax: 602-542-3258
www.revenue.state.az.us

Automatic exemption: No

CHARITABLE SOLICITATION:

Secretary of State
Charitable Organization
1700 West Washington, 7th Floor
Phoenix, AZ 85007-2808
800-458-5842
www.sos.state.az.us

Statute:

Arizona Revised Statutes, Sections 44-1522, 44-6551 *et seq.*

Exemption: first $25,000 or 10 or less donors

Annual filing: Yes

Accept URS: No

Arkansas

INCORPORATION:

Secretary of State
Business and Commercial Services Division
Ste. 250 of the Victory Building
1401 West Capitol Ave.
Little Rock, AR 72201
501-682-3409
888-233-0325
www.sosweb.state.ar.us/corp_ucc.html

What they supply:

State sends material within two weeks. State provides one copy of fill-in-the-blanks Articles of Incorporation and Registration Process sheet.

What must be filed:

Complete both copies of the fill-in-the-blanks Articles and file them with the Secretary of State. Make sure that the Articles are signed by all incorporators.

Name requirements:

The corporate name may not contain a word or phrase that indicates that it is organized for a purpose other than one or more of the purposes contained in your Articles of Incorporation. It has to contain "corporation," "incorporated," "company" or an abbreviation. Note: Name may not end in "company" if preceded by "and".

Director requirements:

Your corporation must have at least three directors. The directors don't have to be residents of Arkansas.

Article requirements:

The minimum requirements for the Articles are as follows:

- the name of the corporation
- the determination whether the corporation shall be a public-benefit, a mutual-benefit or a religious corporation
- a statement whether or not the corporation will have members
- if applicable, provisions regarding the distribution of assets on dissolution
- the street address and the name of the corporation's initial registered office
- the address and signature of each incorporator

Filing fees:

$50, payable to the Secretary of State. For online filing, add a processing fee of $5.00.

Reports: Not required

Statute: Arkansas Code, Title 4, Sec. 28-206

TAXES:

Department of Finance and Administration
P.O.Box 1272,
Rm. G10, Ledbetter Bldg
Little Rock, AR 72203-0919
501-682-7020
Fax: 501-682-4574
www.accessarkansas.org/dfa

Automatic exemption: No

CHARITABLE SOLICITATION:

Office of the Attorney General
Consumer Protection Division
323 Center Street, Suite 200
Little Rock, AR 72201
501-682-1109
800-482-8982

Statute: Arkansas Code, Title 4, Sec. 28-406

Exemption:

$10,000, provided all fundraising activities are carried out by volunteers.

Annual filing: Yes

Accept URS: Yes

California

INCORPORATION:

Secretary of State
Corporations
1500 11th Street
Sacramento, CA 95814
916-657-5448
www.ss.ca.gov/business/corp/corporate.htm

What they supply:

State provides sample Articles of Incorporation for religious, public benefit, and mutual benefit nonprofits with instructions. They also provide a booklet with tax exemption application forms (form FTB 3500). State sends material within two weeks.

What must be filed:

Draft your own Articles accordingly to the applicable sample Articles provided by the state. The documents must be typed in black ink on one side of the paper only.

To avoid the initial annual franchise tax of $800 complete the application form for exemption from franchise tax (form 3500), enclose all attachments called for in the instructions, and file this application together with the original and four copies of your Articles. Also enclose the $25 application filing fee, the state filing fee, and a self-addressed envelope. The Secretary of State will certify two copies without charge. Any additional copies will be certified upon request and payment of $8.00 per copy.

Name requirements:

The following words are not allowed in the corporation's name: "bank", "trust", or "trustee." The name shall not be the same or deceptively similar to the name or any other corporation existing in California.

Director requirements:

Your nonprofit corporation must have at least one director. The directors do not have to be residents of California.

Articles requirement:

Your Articles must have the following minimum contents:

- the corporate name
- the general purpose (Mutual Benefit Corporation, Public Benefit Corporation, Religious Corporation) and the specific purpose of the corporation
- name and California street address of the initial agent (post office box alone is not acceptable)
- signature and typed name (directly below the signature) of at least one incorporator
- if directors are stated in the Articles, each named person must acknowledge and sign the Articles
- special statements required to be included in the Articles to get the tax exemption (only where applicable—please contact the Franchise Tax Board under the address typed below)

Filing fees:

$30, for expedited processing of documents, add a special handling fee of $15. The special handling fee must be remitted by a separate check and will be retained whether documents are filed or rejected.

Reports:

You have to file an annual report within 120 days of the end of corporation's fiscal year.

Statute:

California Code, Nonprofit Corporation Law, Public Benefit Corporations, Section 5122

TAXES:

Franchise Tax Board
P.O. Box 942840
Sacramento, CA 94257-0600
800-852-5711
www.ftb.ca.gov

Automatic exemption: No

CHARITABLE SOLICITATION:

State of California
Office of the Attorney General
P.O. Box 903447
Sacramento, CA 94203-4470
916-445-2021

Statute:

California Government Code Sec. 12580-12596; California Code of Regulations, Title 11, 300-310, 999.1-999.4; California Business and Professional Code Sec. 17510-17510.85; 22930; California Corporation Code Sec. 5223-5250

Exemption: $25,000

Annual filing: Yes

Accept URS: Yes

Colorado

INCORPORATION:

Secretary of State
Corporations Office
1560 Broadway, Ste. 200
Denver, CO 80202-5169
303-894-2200
Fax: 303-869-4864
www.sos.state.co.us/pubs/business/main.htm

What they supply:

State sends material within one week. State sends you fill-in-the-blanks Articles of Incorporation with instructions on how to use the website.

What must be filed:

Make a copy of the fill-in-the-blanks Articles and complete both documents by typing them in black ink. File both originals and enclose the filing fee. Include a typed or machine printed self-addressed envelope.

Name requirements:

By law the corporate name may not include any word or phrase that implies a purpose not included in the Articles of Incorporation. But because the law doesn't require your Articles to state a certain purpose, the Secretary of State will accept any name that is not deceptively similar to any other domestic corporation already on file with the Secretary of State.

It is not necessary to use a *corporate ending* (*e.g.* Corporation, Co. or Incorporated).

Directors requirements:

Your company must have at least one director and one officer. They do not have to be residents of Colorado.

Articles requirements:

The minimum requirements for a Colorado nonprofit corporation are as follows:

- the corporate name
- the name and street address of the corporation's registered agent and office
- the name and address of each incorporator
- a statement whether or not the corporation will have members
- provisions regarding distribution of assets upon dissolution
- the number of directors your corporation shall have

Make sure that each incorporator listed signs the Articles.

Filing fees:

$50, payable to the Secretary of State

Reports:

You have to file reports every two years (between January 1 and May 1).

Statute:

Colorado Revised Statutes, Chapter 7–122 of the *Colorado Nonprofit Corporation Act*

TAXES:

Department of Revenue
Denver Service Center
1375 Sherman St.
Denver, CO 80261
303-866-3091
www.revenue.state.co.us

Automatic exemption: Yes

CHARITABLE SOLICITATION:

State of Colorado
Office of Secretary of State
Licensing Section
1560 Broadway, Suite 200
Denver, CO 80202
303-894-2214

Statute: Colorado Revised Statutes, Title 6, Article 16

Exemption:

None, but you must only register with a solicitation form. There are no specific requirements like annual fees etc.

Annual filing: By campaign—no renewal required

Accept URS: No

Connecticut

INCORPORATION:

Secretary of State
P.O. Box 150470
Hartford, CT 06115-0470
860-509-6212
www.sots.state.ct.us

What they supply:

State sends material within two weeks. State provides all necessary fill-in-the-blanks forms with instructions such as the Certificate of Incorporation, a "First Report" form and a request form for expedited service. Also a fee schedule is provided.

What must be filed:

Type or print your Certificate of Incorporation in black ink. File only the original together with the filing fee.

Name requirements:

Your corporation name must include the words "corporation," "incorporated," or "company," or the abbreviation "corp.," "inc.," or "co." and must be distinguishable from other company names on file with the Secretary of State.

A name reservation can be made for a $30 fee for 120 days using the application form provided by the State.

Directors requirements:

The corporation must have at least three directors. They do not have to be residents of Connecticut.

Articles requirements:

In Article 2 check the appropriate box whether your corporation shall have members and what rights they shall have. Enter the name and address of your registered agent in Article 3 and make sure the agent signs the Acceptance of appointment.

As a nonprofit, nonstock corporation the purpose of your corporation may be "to engage in any lawful act or activity for which corporations may be formed under the Connecticut Revised Non stock corporation Act" (Article 4).

Filing fees:

$40 (includes a $30 statutory franchise tax), payable to the Connecticut Secretary of State

Reports:

The Organization and First Report must be filed within 30 days of the date on which the corporation holds its organization meeting. The filing fee $25.

Statute:

Connecticut General Statutes, Nonstock Corporations, Sec. 33-427

TAXES:

Department of Revenue Services
Taxpayer Services Division
25 Sigourney Street
Hartford, CT 06106-5032
860-297-5962
800-382-9463 (In-State only)
Fax: 860-297-5698
www.ct.gov/drs/site/default.asp

Automatic exemption: Yes

CHARITABLE SOLICITATION:

Public Charities Unit
c/o Office of the Attorney General
P.O. Box 120
Hartford, CT 06141-0120
203-566-5836

Statute:

Connecticut General Statutes, Sec. 21A-190A, *et seq.*

Exemption:

Less than $25,000 annually and not paying anyone primarily to raise funds.

Annual filing: Yes

Accept URS: Yes

Delaware

INCORPORATION:

> State of Delaware
> Department of State
> Division of Corporations
> P.O.Box 898
> Dover, DE 19903
> 302-739-3073
> www.state.de.us/corp

What they supply:

State sends material within two weeks. State provides complete booklet "Incorporate in Delaware" that contains any information about doing business in Delaware. The booklet includes fee schedules, a franchise tax schedule, phone and fax directory, a list of registered agents, and fill-in-the-blanks forms for every kind of corporation.

What must be filed:

Complete the fill-in-the-blanks form Certificate of Incorporation for "nonstock corporations." Print or type your documents in black ink and submit any additional documents in the US letter size "8.5x11". File the original Certificate of Formation and one exact copy. Enclose the filing fee.

Name requirements:

Your corporate name must include one of the following words: "Association," "Company," "Corporation," "Club," "Foundation," "Fund," "Incorporated," "Institute," "Society," "Union," "Syndicate," or one of the abbreviations "Co.," "Corp.," "Inc." A name reservation can be made by calling 900-420-8042 or 900-555-2677. The name will be reserved for 30 days for a fee of $10.

Directors requirements:

Your corporation must have one or more directors. They do not have to be residents of Delaware.

Articles requirements:

Nonprofit corporations must add "This Corporation shall be a nonprofit corporation" in the third Article.
In Article 4 you are asked to state your membership conditions but you can also leave that to be regulated by your Bylaws.

Filing fees:

The filing fee for nonprofit corporations is $50 plus the appropriate county fee of $6.00 for administration and $9.00 per page with a two page minimum.

The fees are payable to the Delaware Secretary of State and can be made by check or credit card.

The Division of Corporations offers expedited service for additional fees:

- Priority 1 (completed within 2 hours of receipt when received by 7:00 pm E.S.T.): $ 500
- same day (when received by 2:00 pm): up to $200
- 24 hour (filing will be completed the next business day): up to $100

Reports:

The annual report has to be submitted to the Division of Corporations in November/December each year. The filing for the annual report is $20.

Statute: Delaware Code Annotated, Title 8, Sec. 102

TAXES:

> Department of Finance
> Division of Revenue
> Carvel State Office Building
> 820 N. French Street
> Wilmington, DE 19801
> 302-577-8205
> Fax: 302-577-8202

> Business Master File Bureau
> 302-577-8250
> www.state.de.us/revenue

Automatic exemption: No

CHARITABLE SOLICITATION:

> Attorney General
> Civil Division
> 820 N. French St.
> Wilmington, DE 19801
> 302-577-8400

Statute: There is no statute requiring registration.

Exemption:

No current registration requirements for solicitation of charitable contributions

Annual filing: No

Accept URS: No

District of Columbia

INCORPORATION:

Department of Consumer and Regulatory Affairs
Corporation Division
941 North Capitol Street, N.E.
Washington, DC 20002
202-442-4432
www.dcra.dc.gov/main.shtm or
http://brc.dc.gov/whattodo/nonprofit/start_
   nonprofit.asp

What they supply:

District sends material within two weeks. Provides one page instructions and fee schedule.

What must be filed:

Draft your own Articles accordingly to the instructions and the sample Articles given by the State. Use plain bond paper, either U.S. letter or legal size. Submit two originally signed and notarized sets of Articles.

Name requirements:

The corporate name may not include language that implies the corporation is organized for purposes other than those stated in the Articles of Incorporation. The name may not be the same or similar to the name of a corporation registered under the law of D.C. and shall not indicate that corporation is organized under an act of Congress. Name reservations can be made for 60 days or a filing fee of $25.00.

Directors requirements:

The corporation must at least have three directors. They do not have to be residents of D.C.

Articles requirements:

The minimum requirements for the Articles are as follows:

- the name of the corporation
- the period of duration (this can be perpetual or a specific period)
- a specific purpose for which the corporation is organized
- a statement whether the corporation shall have members
- if your corporation shall have members, the number of classes of members and the different qualifications and rights of the members of each class
- the manner in which directors shall be elected or appointed and a statement of which class of members shall have the right to elect directors
- a provision of the regulation of the internal affairs of the corporation
- the name of the initial registered agent and the address of the initial registered office
- the number of initial directors the corporation shall have and their names and addresses
- the names and addresses of each incorporator (incorporators must be at least 21 years of age)

Filing fees:

$70, payable to the D.C. Treasurer

Reports:

You have to file a report every two years by January 15.

Statute: D.C. Code, Title 29, Chapter 5

TAXES:

Office of Tax and Revenue
Customer Service Center
941 Capitol St. NE, 1st floor
Washington, DC 20002
202-727-4829
http://cfo.dc.gov/etsc/main.shtm

Automatic exemption: No

CHARITABLE SOLICITATION

Dept. of Consumer & Regulatory Affairs
941 North Capoitol St. N.E.
Washington, DC 20002
202-282-3272

Statute: D.C. Code Sec. 2-711

Exemption: less than $1,500 annually, provided all functions in the corporation are carried out by unpaid persons.

Annual filing: Yes

Accept URS: Yes

Florida

INCORPORATION:

Secretary of State
Division of Corporations
P.O. Box 6327
Tallahassee, FL 32314
800-755-5111
(Non-Profit Articles)
850-245-6052
www.dos.state.fl.us/doc

What they supply:

The state sends the material within one week. State provides a copy of the Florida *Not For Profit Corporation Act*. They also include fill-in-the-blankforms for a nonprofit corporation with specific instructions. Preliminary name searches and name reservations are no longer available from the Division of Corporations. This search can now be made on the Internet at www.sunbiz.org.

What must be filed:

Complete the sample Articles and file the original and one copy. Also complete the transmittal letter provided by the state and attach it to your Articles. Enclose the correct filing fee.

Name requirements:

The corporation name must include one of the words "Corporation," "Corp.," "Incorporated," or "Inc." As a nonprofit corporation you must not use the words "Company" or "Co." You can reserve a name for a fee of $35 for a period of 120 days.

Directors requirements:

There must be at least three directors who must be 18 years of age or older but not need to be residents of Florida.

Articles requirements:

The minimum requirements for the Articles are as follows:

- the name of the corporation
- the principal place of business and mailing address of the corporation
- a specific purpose for which the corporation is formed
- a statement, in which manner the directors are elected or appointed

- the name and Florida street address of your initial registered agent—make sure your registered agent signs the Articles in the space on the bottom page
- the name and signature of each incorporator

Filing fees:

$70 (includes $35 filing fee and $35 for the Designation of the Registered Agent).

For an optional $8.75 plus $1.00 per page of each page over eight, not to exceed a maximum of $52.20, you receive a Certified Copy.

Make your checks payable to the Department of State.

Reports:

The annual report must be filed on or before May 1 each year. The filing fee is $ 61.25.

Statute: Florida Statutes, Chapter 617

TAXES:

Florida Department of Revenue
Taxpayer Services
1379 Blountstown Hwy.
Tallahassee, FL 32304-2716
850-488-6800
800-352-3671
http://sun6.dms.state.fl.us/dor

Automatic exemption: No

CHARITABLE SOLICITATION:

Florida Department of Agriculture
Solicitation of Contributions
P.O. Box 6700
Tallahassee, FL 32314-6700
850-488-2221

Statute: Florida Statutes, Chapter 496

Exemption:

Less than $25,000 carried out by unpaid fundraisers.

Annual filing: Yes

Accept URS: No

Georgia

INCORPORATION:

Secretary of State
Corporations Division
Suite 315, West Tower
#2 Martin Luther King, Jr. Drive, S.E.
Atlanta, GA 30334-1530
404 656-2817
Fax: 404-657-2248
www.sos.state.ga.us/corporations or
www.georgiacorporations.org

What they supply:

The state sends material within one week. State provides sample Articles of Incorporation and instructions to draft your own Articles. Attached is a fill-in-the-blanks "Transmittal Information" form that has to be filed with the Articles.

What must be filed:

Draft your own Articles accordingly to the guidelines given by the state. Submit the original and one exact copy. Also fill in the "Transmittal Information" form and attach it to the Articles. Enclose the filing fee.

Note that all corporations have to publish a notice of intent to incorporate in the official legal newspaper of the county in which the registered office of the corporation is located (the Clerk of Superior Court will give you advice).

You must forward your notice of intent together with a $40 publication fee directly to the newspaper on the next business day after filing your Articles. A sample notice of incorporation is included in the instructions how to draft your Articles.

Name requirements:

A corporate name can and should be reserved prior to filing. A reservation can be made: by faxing a request to 404-651-7842, at the Corporations Divisions website, or by writing to the Division. Reservations are not available by phone. You will receive a name reservation number that remains in effect for 90 days.

Directors requirements:

Your corporation must have at least 3 directors. They do not have to be residents of Georgia.

Articles requirements:

The Articles must contain the following minimum:

- the name of the corporation

- a statement that the corporation is organized pursuant to the Georgia Nonprofit Corporation Code

- the name of the registered agent and the street address of its office in Georgia (a post office box address alone is not acceptable)

- the name and address of each incorporator

- a statement whether the corporation shall have members

- the mailing address of the corporation

- a signature of one of the incorporators named in the Articles

Filing fees:

$100, payable to the Secretary of State

Reports:

You have to file an annual report between January 1 and April 1.

Statute: Georgia Code Annotated, Title 14-2-120, Sec. 2702

TAXES:

Georgia Department of Revenue
Income Tax Division
1800 Century Center Blvd., N.E.
Atlanta, GA 30345-3205
404-417-2400
www2.state.ga.us/Departments/DOR

Automatic exemption: No

CHARITABLE SOLICITATION:

Secretary of State
Business Services & Regulation
Suite 306, West Tower
#2 Martin Luther King, Jr. Dr.
Atlanta, GA 30334
404-656-4910

Statute: Georgia Code Annotated Sec. 43-17-1, *et seq.*

Exemption: Less than $25,000 annually.

Annual filing: Yes

Accept URS: Yes

Hawaii

INCORPORATION:

Department of Commerce and Consumer Affairs
Business Registration Division
Commissioner of Securities
P.O. Box 40
Honolulu, HI 96810
808-586-2744
Fax: 808-586-2733
www.state.hi.us/dcca/breg-seu or
www.businessregistration.com

What they supply:

State sends material within two weeks. State provides fill-in-the-blanks Articles of Incorporation, tax information, and short filing instructions.

What must be filed:

Complete both copies and file them with the Secretary of State. Enclose the filing fee.

Name requirements:

The corporate name may not include language that implies the corporation is organized for purposes other than those stated in the Articles of Incorporation. The name may not be the same or similar to the name of a corporation registered under the law of Hawaii, unless with written consent of the registered name holder, and with added words to distinguish the names.

Directors requirements:

The corporation must at least have three members and also at least one president, one vice-president, one secretary, and one treasurer.

Articles requirements:

The Articles shall set forth the following minimum:

- the name of the corporation
- the address of the corporation's office
- the purpose for which the corporation is organized
- the names and street addresses of the initial directors
- the names and street addresses of the initial officer
- a statement whether the corporation shall have members
- the signature of each incorporator

Filing fees:

$50, payable to the "Department of Commerce and Consumer Affairs," for an extra $50 you get expedited service (filing will be done within five business days, otherwise at least 20 business days).

Reports:

You have to file an annual report between January 1 and March 31.

Statute:

Hawaii Revised Statutes, Title 23, Section 415B-34

TAXES:

State of Hawaii
Department of Taxation
P.O. Box 259
Honolulu, HI 96809-0259
808-587-4242
800-222-3229
Fax: 808-587-1488
www.state.hi.us/tax/tax.html

Automatic exemption: Yes

CHARITABLE SOLICITATION:

Dept. of Commerce and Consumer Affairs
P.O. Box 3469
Honolulu, HI 96801
808-586-2744

Statute:

Hawaii Statutes, Chapter 467B *Solicitation of Funds from the Public*

Exemption:

No current registration requirements for solicitation of charitable contributions.

Annual filing: No

Accept URS: No

Idaho

INCORPORATION:

Secretary of State
700 W. Jefferson, #203
P.O. Box 83720
Boise, ID 83720-0080
208-334-2300
Fax: 208-334-2282
www.idsos.state.id.us/corp/corindex.htm

What they supply:

The state sends material within one week. The state sends you one copy of fill-in-the-blank Articles of Incorporation and instructions.

What must be filed:

Fill-in forms are provided by the state. File the original and one exact copy together with the filing fee.

Name requirements:

Your company name must contain the words "corporation," "company," "incorporated," or "limited" or an abbreviation of these words.

You can reserve a name by filing an application with the Secretary of State. If the name is available it will be reserved for a period of four months for a fee of $20.

Directors requirements:

The corporation must have at least three directors, but if the corporation is going to be a *religious* corporation your board of directors needs only one person.

Articles requirements:

The Articles must contain the following minimum requirements:

- the name of the corporation
- the purpose for which the corporation is formed (this can be to transact any and all lawful activity for which a nonprofit corporation can be formed)
- the names and addresses of the initial directors
- the name of the initial registered agent and the address of the registered office
- the name and address of each incorporator
- a statement whether or not the corporation shall have members
- any other provision regarding the distribution of assets on dissolution

Make sure that each incorporator signs the Articles.

Filing fees:

$30, payable to the Secretary of State. If expedited service is requested, add $20.00 to the filing fee.

Reports:

During the first year there is no annual report needed. The first and all subsequent annual reports shall be delivered to the secretary of state each year before the end of the month during which your corporation was initially incorporated. [Idaho Statutes, Title 30, Chapter 3, Sec. 136]

There is no fee for filing the annual report.

Statute:

Idaho Statutes, Title 30, Chapter 3 *Idaho Nonprofit Corporation Act*

TAXES:

State Tax Commission
Department of Revenue and Taxation
P.O. Box 36
Boise, ID 83772-0410
208-334-7660
800-972-7660
www.state.id.us/tax

Automatic exemption: Yes

CHARITABLE SOLICITATION:

State of Idaho
Office of Attorney General
700 West Jefferson St.
P.O. Box 83720
Boise, ID 83720
208-334-2400

Statute:

Idaho Statutes, Title 48, Chapter 10 *Charitable Solicitation Act*, and Chapter 12, *Telephone Solicitation Act*)

Exemption:

No current registration requirements for solicitation of charitable contributions.

Illinois

INCORPORATION:

Secretary of State
Business Services Dept.
Springfield Office
Michael J. Howlett Bldg.
501 S. Second St., Room 328
Springfield, IL 62756
217-782-6961

Chicago Office
17 N. State, Suite 1137
Chicago, IL 60602
312-793-3380
www.sos.state.il.us/departments/business_
services/home.html

What they supply:

State sends material within two weeks. State provides fill-in-the-blanks Articles of Incorporation in duplicate and a booklet containing information how to file your Articles.

What must be filed:

Type or print your documents in black ink and file the original and one exact copy. Enclose the filing fee.

After you receive the certificate and your file stamped Articles from the Secretary of State, you must file them with the office of the Recorder of Deeds of the county in which your registered office is located. The recording must be within 15 days after receiving your certificate.

Name requirements:

Your corporate name may not contain words regarding any political party. It must be distinguishable from any other Illinois corporation on file with the Secretary of State. Select a name that does not indicate that your corporation is a corporation for profit.

For name availability call 217-782-9520 prior to filing. A name reservation can be made by a written request listing the name wanted and a brief description of the corporate purpose. The fee is $25.

Directors requirements:

The company must at least have three directors, who do not have to be residents or corporation members.

Articles requirements:

The purpose for which the corporation is formed (Article 4) must be a specific purpose and may not be too general or broad. A list of allowable purposes can be found in the booklet provided by the state (see page 3 of the booklet). Also in Article 4 check the appropriate box whether your corporation shall be a Condominium Association or whether your corporation shall be Cooperative Housing or Homeowner's Association.

Filing fees:

$50, payable to the Secretary of State.

Reports:

The annual report is due before the first day of the corporation's anniversary month each year. The forms will be sent to your registered agent approximately sixty (60) days before the due date.

Statute:

Illinois Compiled Statutes Chapter 805, Act 105, 1992, *The General Not For Profit Corporation Act of 1986*

TAXES:

Illinois Department of Revenue
Willard Ice Building
101 W. Jefferson St.
Springfield, IL 62702
217-782-3336
800-732-8866

James R. Thompson Center
100 West Randolph St.
Chicago, IL 60601-3274
www.revenue.state.il.us

Automatic exemption: Yes

CHARITABLE SOLICITATION:

Charitable Trusts and Solicitation Division
100 West Randolph, 11th Floor
Chicago, IL 60601-3175
312-814-2595

Statute: Illinois Compiled Statutes, Chapter 760, Act 55/1; Illinois Compiled Statutes, Chapter 225, Act 460/1

Exemption:

Corporations with gross revenue less than $15,000 and unpaid fundraisers are required to register but are exempt from annual financial filing.

Annual filing: Yes

Accept URS: Yes

Indiana

INCORPORATION:

Secretary of State
Business Services Division
302 W. Washington, Room E018
Indianapolis, IN 46204
317-232-6576
www.IN.gov/ai/business

What they supply:

State provides one copy of fill-in-the-blanks Articles of Incorporation with brief instructions. State sends material within about two weeks.

What must be filed:

Type or print all three copies of the fill-in-the-blanks forms and file them with the Secretary of State. Enclose the filing fee.

Name requirements:

The corporate name must include one of the words "Corporation," "Incorporated," "Limited," or "Company" or any abbreviation of these words.

Directors requirements:

The corporation must have at least three directors. They do not have to be residents of Indiana.

Article requirements:

In Article 3 check the appropriate box whether the corporation is a public benefit, a religious, or a mutual benefit corporation. Also check in Article 5 whether the corporation will have members. Make sure that the Articles are signed by each incorporator.

Filing fees:

$30, payable to the Secretary of State

Reports:

Nonprofit corporations have to file annual reports with a $10 filing fee.

Statute:

Indiana Code Sec. 23-17 *Indiana Nonprofit Corporation Act of 1991*

TAXES:

Department of Revenue
100 N. Senate Ave.
Indianapolis, IN 46204-2253
317-615-2662
www.in.gov/dor

Automatic exemption: No

CHARITABLE SOLICITATION:

Office of Indiana Attorney General
Consumer Protection Division
Indiana Government Center South, 5th floor
402 W. Washington St
Indianapolis, IN 46204-2770
317-232-6330

Statute: Indiana Code 23-7, Chapter 8

Exemption:

No current registration requirements for solicitations of charitable contributions.

Annual filing: No

Accept URS: No

Iowa

INCORPORATION:

Secretary of State
Corporations Division
1st floor, Lucas Building
321 E. 12th St
Des Moines, IA 50319-1002
515-281-5204
Fax: 515-242-5953
www.sos.state.ia.us/business/nonprofcorp.html

What they supply:

State provides sample Articles of incorporation and a short summary of the *Iowa Nonprofit Corporation Act.*

What must be filed:

Draft your own Articles of Incorporation accordingly to the guidelines and Section 504A.29 of the *Iowa Nonprofit Corporation Act.* See "Articles Requirements" below for details. Deliver the original document and one exact copy together with the filing fee.

Name requirements:

The corporate name may not include language that implies the corporation is organized for purposes other than those stated in the Articles of Incorporation. The name may not be the same or similar to the name of a corporation registered under the law of Iowa.

Directors requirements:

Your corporation must have at least one director who does not have to be a resident of Iowa.

Article requirements:

The Articles must include the following minimum:
- the name of the corporation and the Chapter of the Code under which incorporated
- if you want your corporation to be formed for a limited time the period of duration, skip that if it shall be perpetual
- the purpose for which the organization is organized (must be a charitable, literary, educational, or scientific purpose)
- any provisions that set forth the regulation of the internal affairs of the corporation, including provisions of the distribution of assets upon dissolution
- the name of the registered agent and the address of the initial registered office

- the number and the names and addresses of the initial directors
- if applicable, any provision limiting any of the corporate powers
- the date on which the corporate existence shall begin (not more than ninety days in the future)—you can skip this, your corporation will then exist from the date the state issues the certificate of incorporation
- the name and address of each incorporator

Make sure that the person executing the documents signs and states his or her name and capacity in which he or she signs.

Filing fees:

$20, payable to the Secretary of State

Reports:

You have to file an annual report between January 1 and March 31.

Statutes: Iowa Code Sec. 504A.29

TAXES:

Iowa Department of Revenue
Taxpayer Services
P.O. Box 10457
Des Moines, IA 50306-0457
515-281-3114 (Des Moines or out of State)
800-367-3388 (In-State, Quad Cities, Omaha)
Fax: 515-242-6487
www.state.ia.us/government/drf/index.html

Automatic exemption: No

CHARITABLE SOLICITATION:

Attorney General
Consumer Protection Division
Hoover State Building
1305 East Walnut
Des Moines, IA 50319
515-281-5926

Statute: Iowa Code Chapter 13C

Exemption:

No current registration requirements for solicitation of charitable contributions.

Annual filing: No

Accept URS: No

Kansas

INCORPORATION:

Secretary of State
Corporation Division
1st Floor, Memorial Hall
120 SW 10th Ave.
Topeka, KS 66612-1594
785-296-4564
www.kssos.org

What they supply:

State provides fill-in-the-blanks Articles of Incorporation with filing instructions. State sends all material within one week.

What must be filed:

Complete the fill-in-the-blanks form and file the original and one exact copy. Note that the Articles of Incorporation must be notarized. Enclose the filing fee.

Name requirements:

The corporation's name must include one of the following words indicating a corporation "Incorporated," "Inc.," "Association," "Church," "Club," "Foundation," "Fund," "Institute or Society." It must be different from any corporation's name already existing in Kansas.

Directors requirements:

Your corporation must have at least three directors. They do not have to be residents of Kansas.

Articles requirements:

The purpose your corporation is formed for must be stated in Article 3, a general statement that the purpose is to "engage in any lawful act or activity for which nonprofit corporations may be organized under the Kansas General Corporation Code" is sufficient. You should check with the IRS prior to filing whether your purpose must be specific one.

If you want to apply for the federal tax exempt status you must check the "No" box in Article 4 to make clear that your corporation won't issue capital stock.

Enter the names and mailing addresses of the persons serving as initial directors until the first annual meeting. Make sure the incorporator (minimum of one) signs the Articles.

Filing fees:

$20, payable to the Secretary of State

Reports:

Your corporation must file an annual report with an annual privilege fee (ask Secretary of State for actual fee; fee right now is $20.00). The report form will be send to the registered office prior to the due date. The first report will not be required until your corporation is at least six months old. It is due the 15th day of the sixth month following the close of the corporation's fiscal year.

Statute: Kansas Statutes Annotated, Sec. 17-6002, *Corporations*

TAXES:

Kansas Department of Revenue
Docking State Office Building
Room 150
915 S.W. Harrison St.
Topeka, KS 66612
785-368-8222
877-526-7738 (Outside of Topeka)
Fax: 785-291-3614
www.ink.org/public/kdor

Automatic exemption: Yes

CHARITABLE SOLICITATION:

Secretary of State
Corporate Division
1st Floor, Memorial Hall
120 S.W. 10th Ave.
Topeka, KS 66612-1594
785-296-4564

Statute: Kansas Statutes Annotated, Sec. 17-1760 *et seq.*

Exemption: $10,000

Annual filing: Yes

Accept URS: Yes

Kentucky

INCORPORATION:

Office of the Secretary of State
P.O. Box 718
Frankfort, KY 40602-0718
502-564-3490
Fax: 502-564-5687
www.kysos.com

What they supply:

The state provides material within ten days. State provides fill-in-the-blanks Articles of Incorporation and instructions.

What must be filed:

The Articles must be typewritten or printed and signed by an incorporator if no director has been selected. File the original and two exact copies of your Articles and enclose the correct filing fee.

The Secretary of State will return two "filed" stamped copies to your registered agent's office.

Name requirements:

The corporation name must include the words "corporation" or "incorporated" or the abbreviation "Inc." You can also use the word "company" or the abbreviation "Co." which must not be preceded by the word "and" or the abbreviation "&."

Check the name availability prior to filing by calling 502-564-2848. A name reservation can be made for a fee of $15 for a period of 120 days. You can also check name availability on the Internet.

Directors requirements:

A Kentucky nonprofit corporation must have at least three directors.

Articles requirements:

The minimum requirements for the Articles are as follows:

- the corporate name
- the purpose or purposes for which the corporation is organized
- the name of the initial registered agent and the address of its office
- the mailing address of the corporation's principal office
- the number of the initial directors and the names and mailing addresses of these persons
- the name and mailing address of each incorporator

- any provisions for distribution of assets on dissolution or final liquidation of your corporation

Filing fees:

$8, payable to the Secretary of State

Reports:

You have to file an annual report each June.

Statute:

Kentucky Revised Statutes, Chapter 273

TAXES:

Kentucky Revenue Cabinet
Corporation Income Tax Section
200 Fair Oaks Lane
Frankfort, KY 40620
502-564-4581
www.revenue.ky.gov/kffa2.htm

Automatic exemption: No

CHARITABLE SOLICITATION:

Attorney General's Office
Division of Consumer Protection
1024 Capitol Center Dr.
Frankfort, KY 40601-8204
502-696-5389

Statute: Kentucky Revised Statutes Sec. 367.650

Exemption: None

Annual filing: Yes

Accept URS: Yes

Louisiana

INCORPORATION:

Secretary of State
Corporations Division
P.O. Box 94125
Baton Rouge, LA 70804-9125
225-925-4704
Fax: 225-922-0435
www.sos.louisiana.gov

What they supply:

State sends material within one week. State provides one copy of fill-in-the-blanks Articles of Incorporation with brief instructions.

What must be filed:

To obtain a federal tax identification number call the IRS at 901-546-3920 prior to filing your Articles.

Complete the fill-in-the-blanks form provided by the state. Make sure that your registered agent signs the affidavit on the bottom of the second page. Both Articles and affidavit have to be notarized. File only the original and enclose the filing fee.

Within 30 days after filing your Articles, a multiple original or a copy certified by the Secretary of State and a copy of the Certificate of Incorporation must be filed with the office of the recorder of mortgages in the parish where the corporation's registered office is located.

Name requirements

The name may not be the same or similar to the name of a corporation registered under the law of Louisiana, unless the corporation has failed to do business for two years or to pay franchise taxes for five years. The name may not imply the corporation is an administrative agency and shall not include the following words and phrases: "banking," "banker," "state," "parish," "redevelopment" "corporation," "electric cooperative," "credit union," "assurance," "bank," "building and loan," "casualty," "cooperative," "deposit," "fiduciary," "guarantee," "homestead," "indemnity," "insurance," "mutual," "savings," "security," "surety," or "trust."

Directors requirements:

The corporation must have at least three directors. State the term of office of each director in Article 8.

Articles requirements:

In Article 2 check the first box if you do not want the purpose of the corporation to be limited.

If you want to apply for the federal tax-exempt status you must check "Non-stock basis" in Article 9 to make clear that your corporation does not issue stock. You then have to fill in Article 10, characterizing the qualifications which must be met to be a member of your corporation.

Filing fees:

$60, payable to the Secretary of State

Reports:

You have to file an annual report each year on or before the anniversary date of incorporating in Louisiana. The filing fee is $25.00.

Statute:

Louisiana Revised Statutes, Chapter 12:203

TAXES:

Department of Revenue and Taxation
617 North Third Street
Baton Rouge, LA 70802
225-219-7318
www.rev.state.la.us

Automatic exemption: Yes

CHARITABLE SOLICITATION:

Attorney General
Consumer Protection Division
P.O. Box 94095
Baton Rouge, LA 70804-0201
225-342-7900

Statute: Louisiana Revised Statutes 51:1901-1904

Exemption: None

Annual filing: Yes

Accept URS: Yes

Maine

INCORPORATION:

Office of the Secretary of State
Bureau of Corporation, Elections,
and Commissions
101 State House Station
Augusta, ME 04333-0101
207-624-7752 (Reporting and Information Section)
207-624-7740 (Examining Section)
Fax: 207-287-5874
www.state.me.us/sos/cec or
www.maine.gov/sos/cec/corp/corp.htm

What they supply:

State sends material within two weeks. State provides fill-in-the-blanks forms required to incorporate, including Articles of Incorporation, and an acceptance form for the appointment of the registered agent. Also guidelines on how to complete your Articles and brochures on how to get business advice are provided.

What must be filed:

Type or print your Articles in black ink. Make sure all your documents are dated by month, day and year and all bear original signatures. File the original and attach the completed Acceptance of Appointment as registered agent. Make sure to enclose the correct filing fee.

Name requirements:

You can reserve a corporate name prior to filing by submitting the Application for Reservation of Name form. If available, the name will be reserved for 120 days for a fee of $5.

Directors requirements:

The corporation must have at least three directors. They do not have to be residents of Maine and there are no age restrictions.

Articles requirements:

If you do not want the purpose for which your corporation is formed to be limited just leave Article 2 blank, so that the corporation is organized for all purposes permitted under the law. Enter the number of your initial directors and of the directors to be elected on your first meeting in Article 4 and check the appropriate box in Article 5, whether or not your corporation shall have members.

Articles 6 and 7 are optional, check with the IRS prior to filing your Articles, if your corporation has to meet the requirements stated in Article 7.

Filing fees:

$20, payable to the Deputy Secretary of State

Reports:

The annual report must be filed no later than June 1 the year following the year of incorporation.
Use the Annual Report form issued by the Secretary of State.

Statute: Maine Revisted Statutes Annotated, Title 13-B

TAXES:

Maine Revenue Services
24 State House Station
Augusta, ME 04333-0024
207-287-2076
Fax: 207-624-9694
www.maine.gov/revenue

Automatic exemption: No

CHARITABLE SOLICITATION:

Charitable Solicitations Registrar
State House Station #35
Augusta, ME 04333
207-624-8603

Statute:
9 Maine Revised Statutes Annotated, Title 9,
Sec. 5001-5016

Exemption: $10,000 or 10 or less donors

Annual filing: Yes

Accept URS: Yes

Maryland

INCORPORATION:

State Department of Assessments and Taxation
Corporate Charter Division
301 West Preston Street, 8th Floor
Baltimore, MD 21201-2395
410-767-1184
888-246-5941 (In-State only)
Fax: 410-333-5873
www.dat.state.md.us/sdatweb/charter.html

What they supply:

The state sends the material within ten days. The state sends one copy of fill-in-the-blanks Articles of Incorporation for a tax-exempt nonstock corporation, with guidelines how to draft it and a business checklist.

What must be filed:

Your documents must be typed. File only the original and enclose the filing fee.

Name requirements:

Your corporate name must contain the words "Corporation," "Incorporated," "Limited," "Inc.," "Corp.," or "Ltd." It must be distinguishable from any other corporate name already on file with the Secretary of State.

For name availability, call 410-767-1330 prior to filing.

Directors requirements:

The corporation must have at least one director. The director does not have to be a resident of Maryland.

Articles requirements:

Characterize the purpose for which the corporation is formed with one or two sentences in Article 3 and make sure the purpose is charitable, religious, educational, or scientific.

Enter the minimum and maximum number of directors your corporation shall have and give the name and address of the initial director(s) in the space below.

Filing fees:

$40, payable to the Department of Assessments and Taxation

Reports:

You have to file an annual report by April 15.

Statute:

Annotated Code of Maryland, Corporations and Associations, Sec. 2-104

TAXES:

Comptroller of Maryland
80 Calvert St.
Annapolis, MD 21401
410-260-7980
800-MD-TAXES
www.comp.state.md.us

Automatic exemption: No

CHARITABLE SOLICITATION:

Secretary of State
Charitable Division
State House
Annapolis, MD 21401
410-974-5534

Statute:

Annotated Code of Maryland, Business Regulations Act, Sec. 6-101, *et seq.*

Exemption: $25,000

Annual filing: Yes

Accept URS: Yes

Massachusetts

INCORPORATION:

Secretary of the Commonwealth
Corporations Division
One Ashburton Place, 17th Floor
Boston, MA 02108-1512
617-727-9640
Fax: 617-742-4528
www.state.ma.us/sec/cor/coridx.htm

What they supply:

The state sends material within one week. The State provides fill-in-the-blank Articles of Organization.

What must be filed:

Complete the sample Articles and file the original document with the Secretary of State.

Name requirements:

Your corporate name must include the words "Limited," "Incorporated," or "Corporation" or abbreviations of these words. Religious organizations are exempt from this requirement.

For name availability call 617-727-9640. You can reserve a name prior to filing either by submitting a written application to the Secretary of State or in person. The name will be reserved for thrity (30) days for a fee of $15. The reservation can be renewed once for another $15.

Directors requirements:

The corporation must have at least 3 directors. They don't have to be residents of Massachusetts.

Articles requirements:

The purpose your corporation is formed for can be explained in simple language in Article 2, but if you want to apply for the tax-exempt status, characterize that purpose more specifically in Article 4. Check with the IRS for what requirements must be met to receive the tax-exemption.

Filing fees:

$35, payable to the Commonwealth of Massachusetts

Reports:

The annual report is due before November 1 each year. The filing fee is $15.00.

Statute:

Massachusetts General Laws, Chapter 180

TAXES:

Department of Revenue
Customer Service Bureau
P.O. Box 7010
Boston, MA 02204
617-887-6367
800-392-6089 (In-State only)
www.dor.state.ma.us

Automatic exemption: No

CHARITABLE SOLICITATION:

Department of the Attorney General
Division of Public Charities
One Ashburton Place, 14th Floor
Boston, MA 02108-1698
617-727-2200

Statute:

Massachusetts General Laws, Chapters 12 & 68

Exemption: $5,000 or 10 or less donors

Annual filing: Yes

Accept URS: Yes

Michigan

INCORPORATION:

Michigan Department of Commerce
Corporation and Securities Bureau
Corporation Division
7150 Harris Drive
P.O. Box 30053
Lansing, MI 48909
517-241-6470
Fax: 517-241-0538
www.michigan.gov

What they supply:

State sends material within two weeks. State provides fill-in-the-blank Articles of Incorporation and a "Request for Forms" form.

What must be filed:

Complete the fill-in-the-blanks form by typing or printing legibly in black ink. File only the original document together with the correct filing fee.

Name requirements:

The corporate name may not include language that implies the corporation is organized for purposes other than those stated in the Articles of Incorporation. The name may not be the same or similar to the name of a corporation registered under the law of Michigan, unless the name holder's written consent. Name reservations can be made for 120-240 days at that Bureau of Commercial Services for a $10.00 fee.

Directors requirements:

Your corporation must have at least one director. He does not have to be a resident of Michigan. There are no age restrictions for the directors.

Articles requirements:

Characterize the purpose for which your corporation is formed. This purpose must be specific, a general statement is not sufficient.

Complete either Article III (2) or III (3) depending on whether or not your corporation will issue stock. If you want to apply for the federal tax-exempt status your corporation will be on a non stock basis.

Note that except for educational corporations, which must have at least three incorporators, your corporation must only have one incorporator.

Filing fees:

$20 includes a $10.00 organization fee payable to the State of Michigan

Reports:

You have to file an annually report by October 1. Note that the report must include any distribution of funds to shareholders or members and the amount of loans made to those persons and representatives of your corporation (directors, officers, etc.).

(*Michigan Nonprofit Corporation Act*, 450.2 Sec. 911)

Statutes:

Michigan Compiled Laws, Sec. 21.197/202

TAXES:

Michigan Department of Treasury
Lansing, MI 48922
517-373-3200
www.treas.state.mi.us

Automatic exemption: Yes

CHARITABLE SOLICITATIONS:

Department of the Attorney General
Charitable Trust Section
P.O. Box 30212
Lansing, MI 48909
517-373-1152

Statute: Michigan Compiled Laws Annotated Sec. 400.271

Exemption:

$25,000, provided nobody is paid to fundraise and the financial statements of your corporation are available to the public.

Annual filing: Yes

Accept URS: Yes

Minnesota

INCORPORATION:

> Secretary of State
> Division of Corporations
> 180 State Office Building
> 100 Reverend Dr. Martin Luther King Jr. Blvd.
> St. Paul, MN 55155
> 651-296-2803
> Fax: 651-297-7067
> www.sos.state.mn.us/business/index.html

What they supply:

> State sends material within two weeks. State provides fill-in-the-blank copy of Articles of Incorporation with directions.

What must be filed:

> Print or type your document(s) legibly in black ink. File only the original.

Name requirements:

> Corporate name has to be distinguishable from names of other corporations under the law of Minnesota. Nonprofit corporations can use words indicating that they are incorporated (e.g. "Incorporated," "Corp.," "Corporation," or "Company") but they are not required to use these words.

Directors requirements:

> The corporation must have at least three directors. They do not have to be residents of Minnesota.

Articles requirements:

> Check the "Nonprofit Corporation" box at the top of your Articles. Enter the name of your initial registered agent and the address of its registered office in Article 2. Make sure that each incorporator (minimum of one) signs the Articles.

Filing fees:

> $70, payable to the Secretary of State

Reports:

> The state provides a form, that must be filed during the year.

Statute:

> Minnesota Statutes Annotated Sec. 317A.111

TAXES:

> Minnesota Department of Revenue
> 10 River Park Plaza
> St. Paul, MN 55146
> 612-296-0555
> www.taxes.state.mn.us

Automatic exemption: No

CHARITABLE SOLICITATION:

> Office of Attorney General
> Charities Division
> Suite 1200, NCL Tower
> 445 Minnesota Street
> St. Paul, MN 55101-2131
> 612-296-6172

Statute: Minnesota Statutes, Chapter 309

Exemption: $25,000 annually, provided nobody is paid to fundraise.

Annual filing: Yes

Accept URS: Yes

Mississippi

INCORPORATION:

Secretary of State
Corporations Division
P.O. Box 136
Jackson, MS 39205-0136
601-359-1633
800-256-3494
Fax: 601-359-1607
www.sos.state.ms.us/busserv/busserv.asp

What they supply:

State sends material within one week. State provides computer-readable fill-in-the-blanks forms with detailed instructions how to meet the special requirements for computer-readability. Also a fill-in-the-name Amendment that the corporation is exclusively organized for religious, charitable, scientific, literary, and educational purposes is provided.

What must be filed:

Complete the fill-in-the-blanks form exactly as described in the instructions. File only the original and enclose the filing fee. Attach the completed statement that your corporation is organized only for the purposes that will be recognized for the tax exemption.

Name requirements:

Nonprofit corporation names do not have to include words indicating their corporation status, but they may include such words (e.g. "Corporation," "Incorporated," "Inc.," or "Corp."). A name reservation can be made for a fee of $25.00.

Directors requirements:

The number of directors is not specified in the statutes. You can fix the number of directors in the corporation's Articles or bylaws. The directors do not have to be residents of Mississippi.

Articles requirements:

In Article 4 nonprofit corporations can determine the period of duration, enter either a certain number of years or check "perpetual."
Give the name and address of each incorporator in Article 7.

Filing fees:

$50, payable to the Secretary of State

Reports:

There is no duty to file an annual report. Rather the secretary of state requests an information report.

Statute:

Mississippi Code Annotated Sec. 79-11-137

TAXES:

Mississippi State Tax Commission
P.O. Box 1033
Jackson, MS 39125-1033
601-923-7000
www.mstc.state.ms.us

Automatic exemption: Yes

CHARITABLE SOLICITATION

Secretary of State
Charities Registration
P.O. Box 136
Jackson, MS 39205-0136
601-359-1317

Statute:

Mississippi Code Annotated Sec. 79-11-501 *et seq.*

Exemption:

$4000, provided no one is paid to fundraise.

Annual filing: Yes

Accept URS: Yes

Missouri

INCORPORATION:

Secretary of State
Corporation Division
P.O. Box 778
Jefferson City, MO 65102-0778
573-751-4153
866-223-6535
Fax: 573-751-5841
mosl.sos.state.mo.us/section2.asp

What they supply:

State sends material within ten days. State provides two copies of fill-in-the-blanks Articles of Incorporation with general instructions and with special instructions what requirements have to be met to come within the purview of the federal tax exemption. They also include a fee schedule.

What must be filed:

Complete the fill-in-the-blanks forms and file your Articles in duplicate, make sure both documents are originally signed. Enclose the filing fee.

Name requirements:

The corporate name must be distinguishable from any other company or corporation name already on record with the Secretary of State.

Directors requirements

The corporation must have at least one president and/or chairman, one secretary, and one treasurer.

Articles requirements:

If you want to apply for the tax exempt status, make sure to meet the special requirements listed in the separate instructions. These requirements are as follows:

- the purpose for which the corporation is formed (Article 8) must be a charitable, educational, religious, or scientific one (to meet the state's requirements you also have to indicate exactly what your corporation is doing.)
- the net income of the corporation may not distributed to the member, directors, or other private persons except for reasonable compensation for services rendered
- the corporation may not take part in any political or legislative activities
- upon the dissolution of the corporation the remaining assets must be distributed either for the corporation's purposes or to any other similar corporation qualified as exempt organizations

Filing fees:

$25, payable to the Director of Revenue

Reports:

The annual report, listing the officers and directors of the corporation, is due by August 31st each year but not in the first year of existence. The corporation will not remain in good standing if the report is not filed by November 30th.

Statute:

Missouri Revised Statutes, Chapter 347

TAXES:

Missouri Department of Revenue
Division of Taxation & Collection
301 West High Street, Rm. 330
Jefferson City, MO 65101
314-751-4541
800-877-6881 (forms)
www.dor.state.mo.us

Automatic exemption: Yes

CHARITABLE SOLICITATION:

Attorney General
Supreme Court Building
P.O. Box 899
Jefferson City, MO 65102
314-751-8769

Statute:

Missouri Revised Statutes, Sec. 407.450 *et seq.*

Exemption: None

Annual filing: Yes

Accept URS: Yes

Montana

INCORPORATION:

Secretary of State
P.O. Box 202801
Helena, MT 59620-2801
406-444-2034
Fax: 406-444-3976
www.sos.state.mt.us/css/BSB/contents.asp

What they supply:

State provides two copies of a fill-in-the-blank form with instructions on the back.

What must be filed:

First you have to check if the chosen name of your corporation is available. For this information you have to call the office of the Secretary of State. Then file the fill-in-the-blanks Articles and make a copy of the completed Articles. Mail both documents to the Secretary of State and enclose the filing fee.

Name requirements:

The name may not include language that implies the corporation is created for purposes other than stated in the Articles. It may not be the same or deceptively similar to the name of a corporation under the law of Montana. Last the name may not be fictitiously.

Directors requirements:

The corporation must have at least three directors. They do not have to be residents of Montana

Articles requirements:

Your Articles have to include at least following contents:

* corporate name
* name and address of the registered agent and office in Montana
* name and address of each incorporator
* the specific purpose of the corporation (because the Internal Revenue Service requires specific language in order to qualify for nonprofit tax status it is advised that you contact the IRS)
* a statement whether the corporation will have members
* distribution of assets in the case of dissolution

Filing fees: $20, payable to the Secretary of State. Add an additional $20.00 for priority filing.

Reports:

You have to file an annual report to April 15.

Statute: Montana Revised Statutes Sec. 35-2-202

TAXES:

Department of Revenue
P.O. Box 5805
Helena, MT 59604-5805
406-444-6900
Fax: 406-444-1505 (income taxes)
Fax: 406-444-0629 (business and misc. taxes)
www.state.mt.us/revenue/css/default.asp

Automatic exemption: No

CHARITABLE SOLICITATION:

Secretary of State
Room 225
Capitol Station
Helena, MT 59620
406-444-3665

Statute: Montana Revised Statutes Sec. 35-2-118

Exemption:

No current registration requirements for solicitation of charitable contributions.

Annual filing: No

Accept URS: No

Nebraska

INCORPORATION:

Secretary of State
P.O. Box 94608
Lincoln, NE 68509-4608
402-471-4079
Fax: 402-471-3666
www.sos.state.ne.us/htm/businessmenu.htm or
www.nol.org/business.html (for additional business
and licensing services)

What they supply:

State sends material within one week. State provides a
copy of the statute on nonprofit corporation filings and a
fee schedule.

What must be filed:

You have to draw your own Articles. Follow the
instructions given by the state. The document must be executed by an incorporator. The executing incorporator has
to state her or his name and capacity ("incorporator")
beneath or opposite the signature. Send the original and
one copy to the secretary of state for filing. Make sure that
you enclose the correct filing fee.

Name requirements:

The corporate name may not contain a word or a
phrase that indicates that the corporation is organized for
other than or more of the purposes contained in the
Articles of incorporation. The name may not be the same
or deceptively similar to other registered corporations or
reserved names.

Directors requirements:

The corporation must have at least two directors. They
don't have to be residents of Nebraska.

Articles requirements:

The Articles have to include the following basic contents:

- the corporate name
- a statement about the general purpose of the
  corporation (public benefit corporation, mutual-
  benefit corporation or religious corporation)
- street address (post office box is not acceptable) of
  corporation's registered office and the name of its
  initial registered agent at that office
- name and street address of each incorporator
- a statement whether or not the corporation will
  have members
- provisions not consistent with the law regarding the
  distribution of assets on dissolution

Filing fees:

$10 plus $5 per page recording fee, payable to the
Secretary of State.

Reports:

You have to file an annual report to January 1.

Statute: Nebraska Revised Statutes Chapter 21-1905 *et seq.*

TAXES:

Department of Revenue
P.O. Box 94818
Lincoln, NE 68509-4818
402-471-5729
800-742-7474 (In-State & Iowa only)
Fax: 402-471-5608
www.revenue.state.ne.us/index.html

Automatic exemption: Yes

CHARITABLE SOLICITATION:

Secretary of State
2300 State Capitol
Lincoln, NE 68509
402-471-2554

Statute:

Statutes 28-1440-1446 (unenforceable by a 1996
court decision—check the current status with the Secretary
of State), 28-1447-1449

Exemption: None

Annual filing: No

Accept URS: Yes

Nevada

INCORPORATION:

Secretary of State
Annex Office
202 N. Carson Street
Carson City, NV 89701-4201
775-684-5708
Fax: 775-684-5725
www.sos.state.nv.us/comm_rec/index.htm

What they supply:

State sends material within two weeks. State provides complete "Non-Profit Corporations Filing Packet" that contains fill-in-the-blanks forms of Articles of Incorporation and of a Certificate of Acceptance for the registered agents, filing instructions, and a fee schedule.

What must be filed:

Type or print your Articles in black ink only. File the original and as many copies as you want to be certified and returned to you. Note that you must at least keep one certified copy in the office of your resident agent. Make sure that each incorporator's signature is notarized.

Name requirements:

The corporate name may not appear to be that of a natural person and may not contain a given name or initials unless it is accompanied by one of the words "Corporation," "Corp.," "Incorporated," "Inc.," "Limited," "Ltd.," "Company," or "Co." The name may not be the same or deceptively similar to the name of any other corporation presently on file in Nevada.

For name availability check with the Secretary of State prior to filing by calling 702-687-5203. You can make a name reservation either by email, fax, mail, or in person. Check the name reservation information provided by the state.

Directors requirements:

Choose in Article 4 whether the Governing Board shall be styled as directors or trustees. The Governing Board must at least have one director or trustee. It also needs a president, secretary, and treasurer.

Articles requirements:

Enter the name and address of the initial resident agent in Article 2 and make sure that agent signs the certificate of acceptance on the bottom of the page.

To characterize the purpose for which the corporation is formed in accordance to the IRS requirements check with the IRS prior to filing.

Give the names and addresses of the initial Governing Board in Article 4. Do not forget that each incorporator's signature must be notarized.

Filing fees:

$25. Nevada offers an expedited filing service, which allows 24-hour filing. The additional fee for that service is $100.

Reports:

The fee for the corporation's annual report (annual list of officers and directors) is $15.

Statute: Nevada Revised Statutes Chapter 82

TAXES:

Department of Taxation
1550 E. College Parkway, Suite 115
Carson City, NV 89706
775-684-2000
Fax: 775-684-2020
http://tax.state.nv.us

Automatic exemption:

Yes (state corporate income tax)

CHARITABLE SOLICITATION:

Secretary of State
Capitol Complex
Carson City, NV 89710
702-687-5203

Statute:

Nevada Revised Statutes Chapter 598 and Chapter 692

Exemption:

No current registration requirements for solicitation of charitable contributions.

Annual filing: No

Accept URS: No

New Hampshire

INCORPORATION:

Department of State
Corporate Division
State House, Room 204
107 N. Main St.
Concord, NH 03301-4989
603-271-3244
Fax: 603-271-3247
www.sos.nh.gov/corporate

What they supply:

State sends material within two weeks. State provides fill-in-the-blanks forms of "Articles of Agreement" (three copies) plus filing instructions and statutory excerpts containing the most important statutes for filing the Articles.

What must be filed:

Print or type your documents in black ink and leave 1" margins on both sides.

File the original and one exact copy. Both documents must bear original signatures. Note that your Articles of Agreement must be filed with the clerk of the city or town of the principal place of business *prior* to filing with the Secretary of State. Enclose the filing fee.

Name requirements:

Your corporate name may not be the same or deceptively similar to an existing corporation name. For name availability call 603-271-3246 prior to filing.

Directors requirements:

Note that you need five or more incorporators to form a nonprofit corporation in New Hampshire but only one or more directors.

Articles requirements:

The most important requirement for forming your nonprofit corporation is that you need five or more incorporators.

The legal purposes your corporation may be formed for are listed in Chapter 292:1 of the New Hampshire Revised Statutes.

In Article 7 you have the opportunity to make provisions eliminating or limiting the personal liability of a director or officer of your corporation.

Filing fees:

The filing fee for the filing with the city or town clerk is $5, the fee for filing with the Secretary of State is $25.

Reports:

The corporation must file the first report, called "return," in the year 2005 (regardless of the date of incorporation) and every five years thereafter. The fee for the return is $25.

Statutes:

New Hampshire Revised Statutes Annotated Chapter 292

TAXES:

Department of Revenue Administration
45 Chenell Dr.
P.O. Box 457
Concord, NH 03302-0457
603-271-2191
Fax: 603-271-6121
www.state.nh.us/revenue

Automatic exemption: Yes

CHARITABLE SOLICITATION:

The Attorney General
Registrar of Charitable Trusts
State House Annex
33 Capitol Street
Concord, NH 03301-6397
603-271-2110

Statute: Revised Statutes Annotated Sec. 7:19

Exemption: None

Annual filing: Yes

Accept URS: Yes

New Jersey

INCORPORATION:

New Jersey Division of Revenue
Corporate Filing Unit
P.O. Box 308
Trenton, NJ 08625
609-292-9292
www.state.nj.us/business.shtml

What they supply:

State sends material within two weeks. State provides a booklet about registration for any kind of corporation. It includes fill-in-the-blanks Certificate of Incorporation with filing instructions.

What must be filed:

Type your documents in black ink. File the original and two exact copies. Enclose a self-addressed stamped envelope to receive a filed copy and the correct filing fee.

Name requirements:

Your corporate name must include the words "A New Jersey Nonprofit Corporation," "Corporation," "Incorporated," "Inc.," or "Corp."

For name availability call 609-292-9292 prior to filing, a payment for name reservation can be made by credit card.

Directors requirements:

The first board of directors (trustees) must have at least three members. They do not have to be residents of New Jersey.

Articles requirements:

To obtain the tax exempt status after filing your Articles make sure the purpose for which your corporation is organized (Article 2) will meet the IRS requirements for tax exemption.

You can leave most of the regulation for the corporations inner affairs to your bylaws if you do not want these affairs to be regulated by the Certificate of Incorporation.

Filing fees:

$75, payable to the Department of State. New Jersey offers an expedited service (filing complete within 8.5 hours) for an additional fee of $10. The expedited service request must be delivered either in person or by messenger service (FedEx or UPS—not U.S. Postal Overnight)

Reports:

The annual report form will be mailed to the registered agents office prior to the anniversary date of your corporation.

Statute: New Jersey Statutes Sec. 15A:2-8

TAXES:

New Jersey Division of Revenue
P.O. Box 628
Trenton, NJ 08646-0628
609-292-1730(Business/Tax Registration)
609-292-9292 (Business Services)
www.state.nj.us/treasury/revenue

Automatic exemption: No

CHARITABLE SOLICITATION:

NJ Division of Consumer Affairs
Charities Registration & Investigation
P.O. Box 45021
Newark, NJ 07101
973-504-6262

Statute: New Jersey Statutes Sec. 45:17A *et seq.*

Exemption: None

Annual filing: Yes

Accept URS: Yes

New Mexico

INCORPORATION:

Public Regulation Commission
Corporation Department
P.O. Box 1269
Santa Fe, NM 87504-1269
505-827-4502
800-947-4722 (In-State only)
Fax: 505-827-4387
www.nmprc.state.nm.us/corporations/corpshome.htm

What they supply:

State sends matierial within one week. State provides fill-in-the-blanks forms of Articles of Incorporation and a statement of acceptance of appointment that has to be signed by the initial registered agent. Also filing instructions are provided.

What must be filed:

Type or print your Articles legibly in black ink. File duplicate originals and attach the completed, signed and notarized affidavit of acceptance of your registered agent. Enclose the correct filing fee.

Name requirements:

The corporate name must not be the same or deceptively similar to any other company name already existing in New Mexico.

You can check for name availability by calling the Secretary of State at 505-827-4511.

Directors requirements:

The corporation must have at least three directors. The directors do not have to be residents of New Mexico.

Articles requirements:

The minimum requirements for forming the corporation are as follows:

- the name of the corporation
- the period of its duration, which may be perpetual
- a definition of the purpose for which the corporation is formed
- provisions regulating the internal affairs of the corporation including provisions for distributing remaining assets upon the dissolution of the corporation
- the name of its initial agent and the address of the agent's office
- the number of persons serving as the initial directors and the names and addresses of these directors
- the name and address of each incorporator

Filing fees:

$25, payable to the State Corporation Division. Only checks or cashier's checks are accepted. Certified copies are $10 each, if requested.

Reports:

You must file an annual corporate report due the 15th day of the 5th month after the end of the fiscal year of the corporation. The first report is due within 30 days from date of incorporation in New Mexico.

Statute:

New Mexico Statutes Annotated Chapter 53-8-31

TAXES:

Taxation and Revenue Department
P.O. Box 630
Santa Fe, NM 85709-0630
505-827-0700
Fax: 505-827-0469
www.state.nm.us/tax

Automatic exemption: Yes

CHARITABLE SOLICITATION:

Attorney General of New Mexico
Registrar of Charitable Organizations
P.O. Box 1508
Santa Fe, NM 87504-1508
505-827-6000

Statute:

New Mexico Statutes Annotated, 22:57-22-1 *et seq.*

Exemption: less than $2,500

Annual filing: Yes

Accept URS: Yes

New York

INCORPORATION:

Department of State
Division of Corporations, State Records and Uniform Commercial Code
41 State Street
Albany, NY 12231-0001
518-473-2492
Fax: 518-474-1418
www.dos.state.ny.us/corp/corpwww.html

What they supply:

The state sends material within one week. State provides two copies of a fill-in-the-blanks form Certificate of Incorporation with instructions and law excerpts.

What must be filed:

If you draft your own Articles of Incorporation (not using the forms) make sure that your documents contain a separate page which sets forth the title of the document being submitted and the name and address of the person to which the receipt for filing shall be mailed. Enclose the filing fee.

Name requirements:

Unless corporation is formed for religious purposes, the corporate name must contain the words "corporation," "incorporated," "limited," or an abbreviation of these words. A name reservation can be made for a fee of $10.

Directors requirements:

The corporation must have at least three directors. They do not have to be residents of New York.

Articles requirements:

The Certificate of Incorporation must set forth the following minimum:
- the name of the corporation
- a statement that the corporation is formed pursuant to subparagraph (a)(5) of Section 102 of the Not-For-Profit Corporation Law, the type of corporation it shall be under section 201 (Type A-D), and the purpose for which the corporation is formed
- the county where the corporate office is to be located
- the name and address of each director, if your corporation is an A, B, or C type corporation
- the duration of the corporation, if not perpetual

- a designation of the Secretary of State as agent of the corporation upon whom process may be served and the P.O. address to which the secretary of state shall mail a copy on any process against it served upon him
- if applicable, the name of the registered agent and the address of its initial registered office and a statement that he or she is the agent upon whom process against the corporation may be served
- any provision for the regulation of the internal affairs of the corporation that is not inconsistent with the law (e.g., types or classes of membership, distribution of assets upon dissolution, etc.)

Filing fees:

$75, payable to the Secretary of State. New York offers an expedited service (filing within 24 hours of receipt) for an additional $25—make sure to print "Attention: Expedited Handling" on the envelope.

Reports:

You have to file a report by request of the Secretary of State.

Statute:

New York Not-For-Profit Corporation Law, Sec. 402

TAXES:

State Department of Taxation and Finance
Taxpayer Assistance Center
W.A. Harriman Campus
Albany, NY 12227
800-972-1233
Fax: 518-457-2486
www.tax.state.ny.us

Automatic exemption: No

CHARITABLE SOLICITATION:

Office of the Attorney General
Charities Bureau
120 Broadway, 3rd Floor
New York, NY 10271
212-416-8430

Statute: New York Executive Law Art. 7-A

Exemption: 25,000 and unpaid fundraising

Annual filing: Yes

Accept URS: Yes

North Carolina

INCORPORATION:

Secretary of State
Corporations Division
P.O. Box 29622
Raleigh, NC 27626-0622
919-807-2225
Fax: 919-807-2039
www.secretary.state.nc.us/corporations

What they supply:

State sends material within one week. State provides fill-in-the-blank forms of Articles of Incorporation, Articles of Amendment, and other documents needed for maintaining a corporation. Also a personal note of whom to call for more info on filing.

What must be filed:

Draft your Articles accordingly to the sample and the instructions given in the booklet. File the original and one exact copy together with the filing fee.

After filing the copy will be returned "file-stamped" to the incorporator(s).

Name requirements:

The booklet contains a comprehensive chapter about how to select and determine a corporate name. Your corporate name must be distinguishable from any other corporate name already on record with the Secretary of State. You can call or write to the Secretary of State prior to filing whether the name you want to use is available. A name reservation can be made for a fee of $10.

Directors requirements:

The corporation is required to have at least one director. He or she does not to be a resident of North Carolina.

Articles requirements:

The Articles of Incorporation require the following minimum:

- the corporate name
- a statement, whether the corporation shall be a "charitable or religious corporation" pursuant to the North Carolina. General Statutes Sec. 55A-2-02 (a)(2)
- the name of the initial registered agent and the street address of its initial registered office (if mailing address is different, give the mailing address)
- the name and address of each incorporator (at least one incorporator required)
- a statement whether the corporation shall have members

- provisions regarding the distribution of assets upon the dissolution of the corporation
- the street address (and, if different, the mailing address) and county of the principal office
- the signature and capacity of each incorporator

Filing fees:

$60, payable to the Secretary of State. There's an expedited service available for:

- an additional $ 200 for filing on the same day (documents must be received by 12:00 noon)
- an additional $ 100 for filing within 24 hours

Reports:

An annual report is not required.

Statute:

North Carolina General Statutes, Chapter 55A

TAXES:

Department of Revenue
P.O. Box 25000
Raleigh, NC 27640-0640
877-252-3052
www.dor.state.nc.us

Automatic exemption: No

CHARITABLE SOLICITATION:

State of North Carolina
Department of the Secretary of State
Solicitation Licensing Section
2 S. Salisbury Street
Raleigh, NC 27601
919-807-2214

Statute:

North Carolina General Statutes, Chapter 131F

Exemption:

Less than $25,000 if nobody is paid to fundraise.

Annual filing: Yes

Accept URS: No

North Dakota

INCORPORATION:

Secretary of State
Capitol Building
600 East Boulevard Avenue Dept. 108
Bismarck, ND 58505-0500
701-328-4284
800-352-0867 ext. 8-4284
Fax: 701-328-2992
www.state.nd.us/sec/Business/
businessin/oregmnu.htm

What they supply:

State sends material within two weeks. State provides fill-in-the-blanks form of Articles of Incorporation and a Consent to Serve form to be signed by the registered agent.

What must be filed:

Complete the Articles and file in duplicate. Attach the signed consent to serve and enclose the filing fee for the Articles and for the consent.

Name requirements:

Your corporate name must be distinguishable from any other corporate name already on file with the Secretary of State. The name must not include such words as "bank," "banker," or "banking".

Directors requirements:

The corporation must at least have three directors. They do not have to be residents of North Dakota. Your corporation must have at least two officers: a president and a secretary.

Articles requirements:

The Articles require the following minimum:

- the name of the corporation
- if not perpetual, the duration of its existence
- a specific characterization of the purpose for which the corporation is formed
- provisions for the distribution of assets upon the dissolution or final liquidation of the corporation
- the name of the initial registered agent and the address of the agent's registered office
- the number of your initial directors and their names and addresses

Filing fees:

$30 for filing the Articles, another $ 10 for filing the consent, both fees have to be paid.

Reports:

You must file an annual report by February 1 each year. The first report is due in the year following the starting year of your corporation.

Statute:

North Dakota Century Code Chapter 10-33

TAXES:

Office of State Tax Commissioner
600 E. Boulevard Ave., Dept. 127
Bismarck, ND 58505-0599
701-328-2770 or 800-638-2901
Fax: 701-328-3700
www.state.nd.us/taxdpt

Automatic exemption: Yes

CHARITABLE SOLICITATION:

Secretary of State
State of North Dakota
600 East Boulevard Ave.
Bismarck, ND 58505-0500
701-224-3665

Statute:

North Dakota Century Code Chapter 50-22

Exemption: None

Annual filing: Yes

Accept URS: Yes

Ohio

INCORPORATION:

> Secretary of State
> Corporations Division
> 180 E. Broad Street, 16th Floor
> Columbus, OH 43215
> 877-767-3453
> www.state.oh.us/sos or
> www.sos.state.oh.us/sos/busiserv/index.html

What they supply:

State sends material within ten days. State provides fill-in-the-blanks Articles, a separate form for the registered agent and printed filing instructions from its website, and a booklet on organizing an Ohio business.

What must be filed:

Complete the fill-in-the-blanks Articles and file them with the Secretary of State. Make sure that the Articles are signed by the incorporators and their names are printed or typed beneath their signatures. Enclose the filing fee. The trustees do not have to sign the Articles.

Name requirements:

The name of the corporation is not required to have an corporate ending (*e.g.*, "Inc.," "Corp."). It may not be the same or deceptively similar to another corporation under the law of Ohio.

Directors requirements:

The corporation must have not less than three directors. They do not have to be residents of Ohio.

Articles requirements:

The basic requirements are as follows:

- the corporate name
- the names and addresses of the initial trustees (not fewer than three natural persons)
- name and address of a statutory agent
- the specific purpose of the corporation (a general purpose clause will not be accepted)

Filing fee:

$125, payable to the Secretary of State

Reports:

You have to file an statement of continued existence each five years. You will get a written notice and the necessary forms from the Secretary of State.

Statute: Ohio Revised Code, Chapter 1702.04

TAXES:

> Tax Commissioner's Office
> 30 E. Broad Street, 14th Floor
> Columbus, OH 43266-0418
> 614-846-6712
> www.state.oh.us/tax

Automatic exemption: Yes

CHARITABLE SOLICITATION:

> Ohio Attorney General
> Charitable Foundation Section
> 101 E. Town Street, 4th Floor
> Columbus, OH 43215-5148
> 614-466-3180

Statute: Ohio Revised Code, Chapter 1716

Exemption:

$25,000, provided the corporation does not compensate any person primarily to solicit.

Annual filing: Yes

Accept URS: Yes

Oklahoma

INCORPORATION:

Secretary of State
Corporation Division
2300 N. Lincoln Blvd., Room 101
State Capitol Building
Oklahoma City, OK 73105-4897
405-521-3912
Fax: 405-521-3771
www.sos.state.ok.us/business/business_filing.htm

What they supply:

State sends the material within one week. State provides fill-in-the-blanks Certificate of Incorporation and instructions how to file.

What must be filed:

Type or print your documents clearly and file the original in duplicate. Enclose the filing fee.

Name requirements:

Your corporate name must contain one of the following words or abbreviations: "association," "company," "corporation," "club," "foundation," "fund," "incorporated," "institute," "society," "union," "syndicate," "limited," "co.," "corp.," "inc." or "ltd."

For name availability check with the Corporate Filing Division at 405-522-4560 prior to filing. A corporate name can be reserved by filing a name reservation application with a fee of $10 for a period of sixty days.

Directors requirements:

The corporation must at least have one director or trustee. He or she does not have to be resident of Oklahoma. There needs to be at least three incorporators.

Articles requirements:

The basic requirements are as follows:

- the corporate name
- the name of the initial registered agent and the address of its initial registered office
- if the corporation is a church, the street address of its location
- if not perpetual, the duration of your corporation
- the specific purpose for which the corporation is formed
- the number, names, and mailing addresses of the initial directors
- the names and mailing address of each incorporator

Make sure that each incorporator signs the Articles.

Filing fees:

$25, payable to the Secretary of State

Reports:

You have to file an annual report by March 31.

Statute:

Oklahoma Statutes, Title 18, *Oklahoma General Corporation Act*

TAXES:

Oklahoma Tax Commission
2501 Lincoln Boulevard
Oklahoma City, OK 73194
405-521-1350
www.oktax.state.ok.us

Automatic exemption: Yes

CHARITABLE SOLICITATION:

Secretary of State
101 State Capitol
Oklahoma City, OK 73105
405-521-4274

Statute: Oklahoma Statutes Title 18:552 *et seq.*

Exemption: Less than $10,000

Annual filing: Yes

Accept URS: Yes

Oregon

INCORPORATION:

Secretary of State
Corporation Division
255 Capitol St. NE, Suite 151
Salem, OR 97310-1327
503-986-2200
Fax: 503-378-4381
www.sos.state.or.us/corporation

What they supply:

State provides complete business package, including the "Oregon Business Guide," that gives detailed information on all kinds of businesses. The package also includes tax tables, an Employer's Registration form, and an application for the Employer Identification Number (IRS form SS-4). To obtain more information about nonprofit corporations, call the state's toll-free helpline at 888-206-3076.

What must be filed:

Type or print the Articles in black ink. If you file your documents by mail, attach one exact copy of the original. Enclose the filing fee.

Name requirements:

The corporate name must contain the words "corporation," "incorporated," "company," "limited," or an abbreviation of these words. The name must be distinguishable from other active names on the Business Records.

For name availability call 503-986-2200. For a name reservation send an application and a $10 fee to the filing office. If the name is available, it will be reserved for 120 days.

Directors requirements:

A certain number of directors is not required, but you have to fix the number of initial directors in the Articles and the number of subsequent directors in the bylaws.

Articles requirements:

The basic requirements are as follows:

- corporate name
- name and address of registered agent (the address must be an Oregon street address and identical with the agent's business office, post office boxes are not acceptable)
- additional the agent's mailing address
- corporation's address for mailing notices
- type of corporation (public benefit, mutual benefit, religious)
- a statement whether the corporation will have members or not
- a statement concerning the distribution of assets upon dissolution
- names and addresses of all incorporators

Make sure that each incorporator signs the document and print or typewrite the names beneath the signatures.

Filing fees:

$20 for filing the Articles, payable to the "Corporation Division." Fees can be paid by check or by Visa or Mastercard.

Reports:

The annual report must be delivered to the secretary of state on the anniversary date of your corporation. The annual report form is sent to the registered agent forty-five days prior to the due date. The annual fee is $10.

Statute:

Oregon Revised Statutes, Chapter 65 *Oregon Business Corporation Act*

TAXES:

Department of Revenue
955 Center St. NE
Salem, OR 97301-2555
503-378-5988
800-356-4222 (In-State only)
www.dor.state.or.us

Automatic exemption: Yes

CHARITABLE SOLICITATION:

Oregon, Dept. of Justice
Charitable Activities Section
1515 S.W. 5th Avenue, Suite 410
Portland, OR 97201-5451
503-229-5725

Statute: Oregon Revised Statutes Sec. 128.610–129

Exemption: None

Annual filing: Yes

Accept URS: Yes

Pennsylvania

INCORPORATION:

Department of State
Corporation Bureau
210 North Office Building
Harrisburg, PA 17120
717-787-1057
www.dos.state.pa.us/corps/site/default.asp

What they supply:

State sends material within ten days. The state provides fill-in-the-blanks Articles of Incorporation with filing instructions and a fill-in-the-blanks docketing statement that has to be filed with your Articles.

What must be filed:

Print or type your documents in black or blue-black ink. File the original of your Articles of Incorporation, attach a cover letter and enclose the following:

- one copy of the completed docketing statement (form DSCB: 15-134A)—this form is provided by the state
- if applicable, copies of the Consent to Appropriation of Name or, copies of the Consent to Use of Similar Name
- the filing fee

Also include either a self-addressed, stamped postcard with the filing information noted or a self-addressed, stamped envelope with a copy of the filing document to receive confirmation of the file date prior to receiving the microfilmed original.

Name requirements:

The corporate name must include the words "incorporated," "corporation," "company," "limited," "fund," "association," "syndicate," or an abbreviation of these words.

Name availability can be checked either by a written request or by phone at 717-787-1057. The fee for an availability of three names is $12.

A name reservation can only be made by a written request together with a $52 fee. The reservation is good for 120 days. You will get a confirmation of your reservation by mail.

Directors requirements:

If you do not specify the number of directors in your bylaws, the minimum number is three, otherwise one.

Articles requirements:

If you want to apply for the federal tax exemption, check with the IRS prior to filing your Articles to make sure your corporation meets the special purpose required to qualify for the tax exemption (purpose must be given in Article 3).

Give the name and address of each incorporator in Article 8 (minimum of one incorporator).

Filing fees: $100, payable to the Department of State

Reports:

An annual report must only be filed if there is any change of the corporation's officers. If your corporation must file such a report, there is no filing fee.

Statute: Pennsylvania Consolidated Statutes Title 15

TAXES:

Department of Revenue
Bureau of Corporation Taxes
P.O. Box 8911
Harrisburg, PA 17127
717-787-1064
www.revenue.state.pa.us

Automatic exemption: No

CHARITABLE SOLICITATION:

Department of State
Bureau of Charitable Organizations
P.O. Box 8723
Harrisburg, PA 17120
717-783-1720

Statute: Pennsylvania Consolidated States Secs. 10-621.1 *et seq.*

Exemption:

Less than $25,000 annually, provided nobody is paid to fundraise.

Annual filing: Yes

Accept URS: Yes

Rhode Island

INCORPORATION:

Office of the Secretary of State
Corporations Division
100 N. Main Street, 1st Floor
Providence, RI 02903-1335
401-222-3040
Fax: 401-222-1309
www.corps.state.ri.us/corporations.htm

What they supply:

State sends material within two weeks. State provides original and duplicate fill-in-the-blanks Articles of Incorporation with filing instructions.

What must be filed:

Complete and sign the original and the duplicate Articles. Enclose the filing fee.

When the Articles are properly completed, a Certificate of Incorporation, together with the file stamped original will be returned to you.

Name requirements:

The name may not be the same or deceptively similar to any other entity name already on file with the Corporations Division.

For name availability check prior to filing by calling the Corporations Division at 717-783-6035

Directors requirements:

The corporation must have at least three directors. They do not have to be residents of Rhode Island.

Articles requirements:

The minimum requirements are as follows:

- the corporate name
- if not perpetual, the duration of the corporation
- the specific purpose your corporation is formed for (if you want to apply for the federal tax exemption, check with the IRS prior to filing if your corporation must meet specific requirements)
- any provisions for regulating the corporation's internal affairs
- the name of the initial registered agent and the address of its initial registered office
- the number of directors and their names and addresses
- the name and address of each incorporator

Make sure that each incorporator signs the Articles.

Filing fees:

$35, payable to the Secretary of State

Reports:

An annual report must be filed each calendar year in the month of June beginning the year following the year of incorporation.

Statute:

General Laws Rhode Island Chapter 7-6-34

TAXES:

Rhode Island Division of Taxation
One Capitol Hill
Providence, RI 02908
401-277-2905
Fax: 401-277-6006
www.tax.state.ri.us

Automatic exemption: Yes

CHARITABLE SOLICITATION:

State of Rhode Island
Department of Business Regulation
Charitable Organizations Section
233 Richmond Street, Suite 232
Providence, RI 02903-4232
401-222-3048

Statute: Rhode Island Genereal Laws Title 5, Chapter 53

Exemption: $3000 or 10 or less donors in a year

Annual filing: Yes

Accept URS: Yes

South Carolina

INCORPORATION:

Secretary of State
P.O. Box 11350
Columbia, SC 29211
803-734-2158
www.scsos.com/corporations.htm

What they supply:

State sends material within one week. State provides fill-in-the-blanks Articles of Incorporation with brief instructions.

What must be filed:

File the completed original and either a duplicate original or a conformed copy. Enclose the filing fee.

Name requirements:

The corporate name must include the words "corporation," "incorporated," "company," "limited," or an abbreviation of these words. It must be distinguishable from any other business name already on file with the Secretary of State.

A name can be reserved for 120 days for a fee of $25.

Directors requirements:

Your corporation must have at least one director. He or she does not have to be a resident of South Carolina.

Articles requirements:

In Article 3 check the appropriate box whether the corporation is a public benefit, religious, or mutual benefit corporation. If you want to apply for the federal tax exemption and your corporation is either a public benefit or religious corporation, check the "a" box in Article 6 to make sure that upon dissolution of the corporation, the assets will be distributed accordingly to the tax exempt purposes. If you form a mutual benefit corporation check one of the two dissolution statements in Article 7.

Each incorporator (minimum of one) must sign the Articles.

Filing fees:

$25, payable to the Secretary of State.

Reports:

You have to file an annual report by the 15th day of the 3rd month after the end of the corporation's fiscal year.

Statute:

South Carolina Code Annotated Chapter 33-44

TAXES:

South Carolina Tax Commission
P.O. Box 125
Columbia, SC 29214
803-898-5000
Fax: 803-898-5822
www.sctax.org

Automatic exemption: Yes

CHARITABLE SOLICITATION:

Secretary of State
Public Charities Division
P.O. Box 11350
Columbia, SC 29211
803-734-1790

Statute: South Carolina Code Annotated 33-56-10

Exemption: $5,000

Annual filing: Yes

Accept URS: Yes

South Dakota

INCORPORATION:

Secretary of State
State Capitol, Suite 204
500 E. Capitol Ave.
Pierre, SD 57501-5070
605-773-4845
Fax: 605-773-4550
www.state.sd.us

What they supply:

State sends material within one week. State provides fill-in-the-blanks-form of Articles of Incorporation.

What must be filed:

Type the Articles and file the original document and one exact copy. Make sure that the consent of appointment is signed by the registered agent and that the Articles are notarized. Enclose the filing fee.

Name requirements:

The corporate name may not be the same or deceptively similar to the name of any other corporation registered in the State of South Dakota.

For name availability check with the Secretary of State at 605-773-4845. A name can be reserved for a period of 120 days for a fee of $15.

Directors requirements:

The board of directors must have at least three members. The directors do not have to be residents of South Dakota.

Articles requirements:

The Articles must contain the following minimum:
- the name of the corporation
- if not perpetual, the period of existence
- the purpose for which the corporation is formed—this clause must contain sufficient information to determine the type of purpose. Types of purposes are given in Section 47-22-4 of the statutes.
- a statement whether the corporation shall have mem   bers and if so, provisions regulating the class of members and their rights
- regulations concerning the method of election of the directors
- any provisions regulating the internal affairs of the corporation

- the street address of your initial registered office and the name or your initial registered agent
- the number of directors and their names and addresses
- the names and addresses of the incorporators (minimum of three)
- the signature of each incorporator

Filing fees:

$25, payable to the Secretary of State

Reports:

A report containing the basic information about your corporation has to be filed every three years by the first day of the second month following the anniversary month of the corporation. The Secretary of State will provide forms for filing this report prior to the due date. The filing fee for the report is $10.

Statute:

South Dakota Codified Laws Chapter 47

TAXES:

Department of Revenue and Regulation
445 East Capitol Ave.
Pierre, SD 57501-3100
605-773-3311
800-TAX-9188
Fax: 605-773-5129
www.state.sd.us/drr2/revenue.html

Automatic exemption: Yes

CHARITABLE SOLICITATION:

Attorney General
State Capitol
500 East Capitol
Pierre, SD 57501-5070
605-773-4400

Statute:

South Dakota Codified Laws, Title 37, Chapter 30 (regulates only solicitation of charitable contributions by telephone)

Exemption: None

Annual filing: No

Accept URS: No

Tennessee

INCORPORATION:

Secretary of State
Division of Business Services
6th Floor, William R. Snodgrass Tower
312 Eighth Avenue North
Nashville, TN 37243
615-741-2286
Fax: 615-532-9870
www.state.tn.us/sos/service.htm

What they supply:

State sends material within ten days. Provides a comprehensive and detailed "Filing Guide" for Nonprofit Corporations, a filing fee schedule, and a fill-in-the-blanks Charter (Articles of Incorporation).

What must be filed:

Type or print the Articles in black ink using either the fill-in-the-blanks form or, if drafting your own documents, using legal or letter size paper. The documents must be executed either by an incorporator, by the chair of the board of directors, or by a trustee. File only the original document(s) together with the filing fee.

Name requirements:

The corporate name must be distinguishable from any other name on file with the Division of Business Services, the filing guide provides sufficient information, whether or not names are distinguishable from others. It may not contain language implying that the corporation transacts business for which authorization is required or that the corporation is organized as a fraternal, veterans, service, religious, charitable, or professional organization.

For name availability call 615-741-2286 or use the database at the website prior to filing. A name reservation can be made by filing an application with the Division of Business Services together with a $20 fee.

Directors requirements:

The corporation must have at least one director. They do not have to be residents of Tennessee.

Articles requirements:

The charter must contain the following minimum:

- the corporate name
- a statement whether the corporation is a public or mutual benefit corporation or whether it is a religious corporation
- the address of the initial registered office and the name of the initial registered agent
- the name and address of each incorporator
- the street address of the principal office (may be the same as the address of the registered agent)
- a statement that the corporation is not for profit
- a statement that there will be no members
- provisions regarding the distribution of assets upon the dissolution of the corporation

Filing fees:

$100, payable to the Division of Business Services

Reports:

The annual report must be filed on or before the first day of the fourth month following the close of the corporation's fiscal year. The report form will be sent to the registered office one month prior to the end of the corporation's fiscal year. The fee for the annual report is $ 20.

Statute:

Tennessee Code Annotated Section 48-52

TAXES:

Tennessee Department of Revenue
Andrew Jackson Office Bldg.
500 Deaderick Street
Nashville, TN 37242-1099
615-741-3133
Fax: 615-741-0682
www.state.tn.us/revenue

Automatic exemption: Yes

CHARITABLE SOLICITATION:

Department of State
Division of Charitable Solicitations
312 8th Avenue N., 8th Floor
William Snodgrass Tower
Nashville, TN 37243
615-741-2555

Statute: Tennessee Code Annotated Sec. 48-101-501 *et seq.*

Exemption: $30,000

Annual filing: Yes

Accept URS: Yes

Texas

INCORPORATION:

Secretary of State
Statutory Filings Division
Corporations Section
P.O. Box 13697
Austin, TX 78711-3697
512-463-5555
Fax: 512-463-5709
www.sos.state.tx.us/corp/nonprofit.shtml

What they supply:

State sends material within one week. State provides guidelines to draft your own Articles of Incorporation (a so-called "Nonprofit Corporation Summary," form 202) and one copy of fill-in-the-blank Articles of Incorporation.

What must be filed:

Draft your own Articles accordingly to the instructions provided by the state or fill out the form provided. File two copies of these together with the filing fee. The filing office will return one filed stamped copy.

Name requirements:

The corporate name may include words like "corporation," "incorporated," or "company," but it is not mandatory.

For name availability call 512-463-5555 prior to filing. A name reservation can be made for a fee of $25 for a period of 120 days.

Directors requirements:

The corporation may not have less than three directors. They do not have to be residents of Texas.

Articles requirements:

The minimum contents of your Articles are as follows:

- the name of the corporation
- the period of duration, which may be perpetual
- a statement that the corporation is not for profit
- the specific purpose for which the corporation is formed (check with the IRS prior to filing what requirements your corporation has to meet to qualify for the federal tax exemption)
- the name of the registered agent and the address of the registered office.
- a statement whether corporation shall have members

- if the management of the corporation shall be vested in the members, a statement to that effect
- the number of the initial board of directors and the names and addresses of your directors
- the name and street address of each incorporator
- provisions regarding the distribution of assets upon the dissolution of the corporation

Make sure that each incorporator signs the Articles.

Filing fees: $25, payable to the Secretary of State

Reports:

You have to file a report upon request from the Secretary of State (once every four years). The Secretary of State will send notice and the necessary forms before the report is due.

Statute: Texas Non-Profit Corporation Act, Article 1396-3.02

TAXES:

Office of the Comptroller
P.O. Box 13528, Capitol Station
Austin, TX 78711-3528
512-463-4142
www.window.state.tx.us

Automatic exemption: No

CHARITABLE SOLICITATION:

Attorney General
Charitable Trust Section
P.O. Box12548
Austin, TX 78711
512-463-2018

Statute:

Texas does not have a general statute, but certain cities have special requirements for solicitation of charitable contributions.

Exemption:

No current state registration requirements for solicitation of charitable contribution

Annual filing: No

Accept URS: No

Utah

INCORPORATION:

Department of Commerce
Division of Corporations and Commercial Code
P.O. Box 146705
Salt Lake City, UT 84114-6705
801-530-4849
877-526-3994 (In-State only)
www.commerce.utah.gov/cor

What they supply:

The state sends material within ten days. State provides guidelines how to draft your own Articles of organization and sample Articles.

What must be filed:

File one original and one exact copy of your self-drafted Articles. At least one document must bear the original signature. You can deliver the documents personally, by mail, or even by fax. If you choose to fax your documents, make sure to include the number of your Visa/Mastercard and the expiration date.

Name requirements:

There are no special name requirements for your corporate name, although the name may contain the words "corporation" or "incorporated." The corporate name must be distinguishable from any other corporate name already on file with the Secretary of State.

Directors requirements:

The corporation must at least have three trustees. They do not have to be residents of Utah or member of the corporation.

Articles requirements:

The minimum of what the Articles must contain is:
* the corporate name
* the term of the corporation's existence
* the purpose or purposes for which your corporation is formed—this must include the statement that it is organized as a non-profit corporation
* the address of the corporation's principal office
* a statement whether or not the corporation shall have members
* the number of initial trustees your corporation shall have and their names and addresses
* the name and street address of each incorporator (at least one)
* the name of the corporation's initial registered agent and the street address of the registered office
* the signature of each incorporator

The Articles also must include a statement by your registered agent that he or she acknowledges his or her acceptance as registered agent.

Filing fees: $22, payable to the Secretary of State.

Reports:

The annual report must be filed in the month of the anniversary date the corporation was created. The Division of Corporations sends an annual report notice and a reporting form to the registered agent prior to the filing date.

Statute:

Utah Code Annotated, Section 16-6-46
Corporation Laws

TAXES:

Utah State Tax Commission
160 E. 300 S
P.O. Box 4000
Salt Lake City, UT 84134
801-530-4848
www.tax.ex.state.ut.us

Automatic exemption: No

CHARITABLE SOLICITATION:

Department of Commerce
Division of Consumer Protection
160 East 300 South
P.O. Box 146704
Salt Lake City, UT 84114-6704
801-530-6601

Statute:

Utah Code Annotated, Title 13, Chapter 22, Sec. 1-22

Exemption: None

Annual filing: Yes

Accept URS: Yes

Vermont

INCORPORATION:

Office of the Secretary of State
Corporations Division
Heritage One Building
81 River Street, Drawer 09
Montpelier, VT 05609-1104
802-828-2386
Fax: 802-828-2853
www.sec.state.vt.us/corps/corpindex.htm

What they supply:

State sends material within one week. State provides fill-in-the-blanks form of Articles of Incorporation for non-profit corporations with instructions.

What must be filed:

Complete the fill-in-the-blanks form by typewriting or printing. File the original and one exact copy. Enclose the filing fee.

Name requirements:

The corporate name must end with the words "corporation," "incorporated," "company," "limited," or "cooperative" (if applicable).

A name can be reserved for 120 days for a fee of $20.

Directors requirements:

The corporation must have at least three directors, if you form a marketing cooperative, it must have at least five directors.

Articles requirements:

The minimum requirements are as follows:

- the corporate name
- the name of the registered agent
- the street address of the registered office
- if not perpetual, the period of duration
- a statement, whether the corporation shall be a public benefit, mutual benefit, nonprofit corporation, or a cooperative.
- the names and addresses of your initial directors
- if applicable, the names and addresses of your members
- the specific purpose for which your corporation is formed
- provisions regarding the distribution of assets upon the dissolution of the corporation
- signatures and addresses of each incorporator

Filing fees:

$75, payable to the Vermont Secretary of State.

Reports:

Nonprofit corporations must file biennial reports. The Secretary of State will send notice before the report is due. The report is due every two years.

Statute: Vermont Statutes Annotated, Title 11
Nonprofit Corporations

TAXES:

Department of Taxes
Agency of Administration
Pavilion Office Building
Montpelier, VT 05602
802-828-2551
www.state.vt.us/tax

Automatic exemption: No

CHARITABLE SOLICITATION:

Attorney General
Pavilion Office Building
Montpelier, VT 05602
802-828-3171

Statute:

Vermont Statutes Annotated, Chapter 63, Title 9, Sections 2471 *et seq.*

Exemption:

Only the paid solicitor needs to register. Otherwise, there are no current requirements for solicitation.

Annual filing: No

Accept URS: No

Virginia

INCORPORATION:

State Corporation Commission
P.O. Box 1197
Richmond, VA 23218-1197
804-371-9733
Fax: 804-371-9133
www.state.va.us/scc/division/clk/index.htm

What they supply:

State sends one copy of fill-in-the-blank Articles of Incorporation with filing instructions within two weeks.

What must be filed:

For forming a nonprofit corporation take form SCC 819 (nonstock corporation). Typewrite your Articles in black ink. Complete and file only the original form and enclose the filing fee.

Name requirements:

There are no special requirements for your corporate name but it must not be the same or deceptively similar to any other corporate name existing in Virginia.

Directors requirements:

If you want the corporation to have initial directors, the minimum number is one. Each initial director has to be named in the Articles.

Articles requirements:

The minimum requirements for filing the Articles are as follows:

- the corporate name
- a statement whether or not your corporation shall have members and if so, provisions designating the classes of members and their rights
- a statement of the manner in which directors shall be elected or appointed
- the name of the initial registered agent and its status
- the address of your registered office
- optional provisions regarding the purpose for which the corporation is formed. To meet the special requirements for obtaining the federal tax exempt status, check with the IRS prior to filing the Articles for which requirements have to be met
- if the corporation shall have initial directors, state the number of directors and their names and addresses

- the signature and printed name of each incorporator

Filing fees:

$75 (including $50 charter fee and $25 filing fee), payable to the State Corporation Commission (pay by check or similar payment method, no cash accepted)

Reports:

The annual report must be filed between January 1 and April 1 with a small registration fee. The Secretary of State will send a report form prior to the due date.

Statute: Virginia Code Annotated Title 13.1 Chapter 10

TAXES:

Department of Taxation
P.O. Box 6-L
Richmond, VA 23282
Fax: 804-367-2062
www.tax.state.va.us

Automatic exemption: Yes

CHARITABLE SOLICITATION:

Virginia Department of Agriculture and Consumer Affairs
P.O. Box 1163
Richmond, VA 23209
804-786-2042

Statute: Virginia Code Annotated Secs. 57-48 to 57-69

Exemption:

$5,000 provided all corporation's activities are carried out by volunteers.

Annual filing: Yes

Accept URS: Yes

Washington

INCORPORATION:

Secretary of State
Corporations Division
P.O. Box 40234
Olympia, WA 98504-0234
360-753-7115
www.secstate.wa.gov/corps

What they supply:

State sends material within ten days. State provides a single page fill-in-the-blanks form of Articles of Incorporation without any instructions.

What must be filed:

Type or print the document in black ink. Submit the original and one copy together with the filing fee.

An expedited service (filing within 24 hours) is available for an extra $20 fee. If you want the expedited service write "expedited" in bold letters on outside of envelope.

Name requirements:

The corporate name may not contain words like "corporation," "incorporated," "limited," or abbreviations "corp.," "inc.," or "ltd.;" but it may contain designations such as "Association," "Services," or "Committee."

For a fee of $20 you can reserve a corporate name for a period of 180 days.

Directors requirements:

The corporation must have one or more directors. He or she does not have to be resident of Washington.

Articles requirements:

At a minimum, the Articles must contain the following:

- the name of the corporation
- if wanted, a specific effective date of incorporation
- the term of existence
- the purpose for which the corporation is formed
- provisions regulating the distribution of assets upon dissolution of the corporation
- the name and street address of the initial registered agent and a signature by this agent, acknowledging acceptance
- the name and address of each initial director
- the name and address of each incorporator
- the signature of each incorporator

Filing fees: $30, payable to the Secretary of State

Reports:

The annual report has to be filed between January 1 and March 1 each year. The fee is $10. The report form is provided by the Secretary of State.

Statute: Washington Revised Code Chapter 24.03

TAXES:

State Department of Revenue
General Administration Building
AX-02
Olympia, WA 98504-0090
206-753-5540
http://dor.wa.gov/upgrade.asp

Automatic exemption: Yes

CHARITABLE SOLICITATION:

Office of the Secretary of State
Charities Division
505 E Union Avenue, 2nd Floor
P.O. Box 40234
Olympia, WA 98504-02234
206-753-7118

Statute: Washington Revised Code Chapter 19.09 *et seq.*

Exemption:

Less than $25,000, provided all corporation's activities are carried out by unpaid persons.

Annual filing: Yes

Accept URS: Yes

West Virginia

INCORPORATION:

Secretary of State
Business Division
Building 1, Suite 157-K
1900 Kanawha Boulevard East
Charleston, WV 25305-0770
304-558-8000
Fax: 304-558-0900
www.wvsos.com

What they supply:

State sends material within ten days. State provides two copies of fill-in-the-blanks Articles of Incorporation and filing instructions.

What must be filed:

Complete the Articles and file both originals. Make sure that the incorporator(s) file both documents and that the documents are notarized. Enclose the filing fee.

Name requirements:

Your corporate name must include the words "corporation," "company," "limited," "incorporated," or an abbreviation of these words. The name may not contain any word or phrase that implies that it is organized for any purposes other than those contained in the Articles of Incorporation.

Name availability can be checked by calling the Secretary of State at the phone number given above. A name reservation can be made by a written application accompanied by a $15 fee. The reservation is good for 120 days.

Directors requirements:

The corporation must have at least one director. The director does not have to be a resident of West Virginia or a member of the corporation. The corporation needs to have two officers—a president and a secretary.

Articles requirements:

The fill-in-the-blanks form provided by the State is both for stock and non-stock (non-profit) corporations. Check the "non-profit" box in Article 5 to denote your corporation structure. Then state the purpose your corporation is formed for in Article 7 and check the appropriate box whether provisions regulating the internal affairs of the corporation shall be set forth in the bylaws or are attached to the Articles. Give the names and street addresses of the incorporators in Article 10 and the names and number of initial directors in Article 11.

Name at least one person who shall have signature authority on documents filed with the Secretary of State (annual report). The incorporators must sign the Articles. Make sure that the signatures are notarized.

Filing fees:

The registration fee for non-profit corporations is $25. An additional "Attorney-in-fact fee," which depends on the month your Articles will be received by the Secretary of State, is also required. Check the fee schedule to find out about the correct additional fee.

Reports:

Your first annual report must be filed between January 1 and March 31 of the first calendar year succeeding the date of incorporation. Thereafter, the reports are due between January 1 and March 31 each year.

Statute: West Virginia Code Section 31-1-27

TAXES:

West Virginia Tax Department
Taxpayer Service Division
P.O. Drawer 3784
Charleston, WV 25337-3784
800-642-9016 (In-State only)
Fax.: 304-558-2501
www.state.wv.us/taxrev

Automatic exemption: Yes

CHARITABLE SOLICITATION:

Secretary of State
Room 157K, 1900
Kanawha Bldg. East
P.O. Box 1789
Charleston, WV 25305
304-558-6000

Statue: West Virginia Code, Chapter 29, Art. 19

Exemption:

Following organizations provided they do not employ a professional fundraiser and do not receive contributions in excess of $10,000 during a calender year:

- local youth athletic organizations
- community civic or service clubs
- fraternal organizations and labor unions
- local posts, camps, chapters, or similarly designated elements or county units of such elements of bona fide veteran's organizations or auxiliaries that issue charters to such local elements throughout the state
- bona fide organizations of volunteer firemen, ambulance, rescue squads, or auxiliaries

Annual filing: Yes

Accept URS: No

Wisconsin

INCORPORATION:

Department of Financial Institutions
Division of Corporate & Consumer Services
P.O. Box 7846
Madison, WI 53707-7846
608-261-7577
Fax: 608-267-6813
www.wdfi.org/corporations

What they supply:

State sends material within one week. State provides fill-in-the-blanks Articles with instructions. You can also download the forms from the Internet under the address mentioned above.

What must be filed:

Complete the fill-in-the-blanks forms and send the original and one copy to the Department of Financial Institutions. Enclose the filing fee. For expedited service (filing procedure will be completed the next business day), mark your documents "For Expedited Service" and provide an extra $25 for each item. Indicate on the back side of your Articles where the acknowledgement copy of the filed document should be sent.

Name requirements:

The corporate name must include the words "Corporation," "Incorporated," "Limited," or the abbreviation of one of those words.

For name availability, call the filing office prior to filing. A name can be reserved either by calling 608-261-9555 or by a written application. The application must include the name and address of the applicant and the name to be reserved. If the name is available, it will be reserved for 120 days. The reservation fee is $15 for the written application, $30 for the telephone application.

If your first choice is not available, you can provide a second choice name on the reverse side of your Articles.

Directors requirements:

The corporation must have at least three directors. They do not have to be residents of Wisconsin.

Articles requirements:

The minimum requirements are as follows:
- corporate name
- the phrase: "The corporation is organized under Chapter 181 of the Wisconsin Statutes"

- name and address of the registered agent (street address of the agent's office is required, post office box address may be part of the address, but is sufficient alone)
- mailing address of the corporation's principal office (it may be located outside of Wisconsin)
- a statement whether the corporation will have members or not
- name, address, and signature of each incorporator
- name of the person who drafted the document (printed, typewritten or stamped in a legible manner)

Filing fees:

$35 filing fee payable to the Department of Financial Institutions, $16 standard recording fee payable to Register of Deeds (if you append additional pages to the form you have to pay $2 more recording fee for each additional page)

Reports:

You have to file an annual report within the calendar quarter of the anniversary of incorporation. The forms are distributed automatically to the corporation.

Statute: Wisconsin Statutes, Chapter 181

TAXES:

Department of Revenue
P.O. Box 8906
Madison, WI 53708
608-266-2776
www.dor.state.wi.us

Automatic exemption: Yes

CHARITABLE SOLICITATION:

Department of Regulation and Licensing
Charitable Organizations
P.O. Box 8935
Madison, WI 53708-8935
608-267-7132 (for A-L)
608-267-7860 (for M-Z)

Statute: Wisconsin Statutes, Chapter 440, Subchapter 3

Exemption: None

Annual filing: Yes

Accept URS: Yes

Wyoming

INCORPORATION:

Secretary of State
Corporations Division
State Capitol Building, Room 110
200 West 24th St.
Cheyenne, WY 82002-0020
307-777-7311
Fax: 307-777-5339
soswy.state.wy.us/corporat/corporat.htm
email: corporations@state.wy.us

What they supply:

State sends material within one week. State provides fill-in-the-blanks form of Articles of Incorporation and of the "Consent to Appointment by Registered Agent" with instructions how to complete these forms.

What must be filed:

Complete the forms and file the original and one exact copy. The Articles must be accompanied by the written consent to appointment executed by the registered agent. Enclose the filing fee.

Name requirements:

There are no special name requirements although your name may contain words like "corporation," "incorporated," or "company." It must be distinguishable from any other corporate name already on file and may not contain language that implies the corporation was organized for other purposes than those stated in the Articles.

A name can be reserved for a fee of $10.

Directors requirements:

The corporation must have at least three directors. They do not have to be residents of Wyoming.

Articles requirements:

The Articles must contain the following minimum:

- the corporate name
- a statement whether the corporation is a religious, a public benefit or a mutual benefit corporation
- the street address of your corporation's initial registered office and the name of the registered agent
- the name and address of each incorporator
- a statement whether your corporation shall have members
- provisions regarding the distribution of assets upon the dissolution of the corporation

- the date and signature of each incorporator

Don't forget to let your registered agent sign the "Consent to Appointment."

Filing fees:

$25, payable to the Secretary of State

Reports:

The annual report must be filed on the first day of the registration anniversary month. The Secretary of State will send out forms two months prior to the due date. The fee is $25.00.

Statute: Wyoming Statute, Section 17-6-102

TAXES:

Department of Revenue
Herschler Building
122 W. 25th Street
Cheyenne, WY 82002
307-777-5235
http://revenue.state.wy.us

Automatic exemption: Yes

CHARITABLE SOLICITATION:

Secretary of State
Capitol Building
200 W. 24th St.
Cheyenne, WY 82002
307-777-7378

Statute: Wyoming Statutes Sec. 17-19-1501

Exemptions:

No current registration requirements for solicitation of charitable contributions.

Annual filing: No

Accept URS: No

This appendix contains the blank forms that can be used to form a nonprofit corporation. Be sure to read the text of this book and each form before using it. If a form does not fit your situation, you may want to change it or consult an attorney. If you do not understand any of the forms, consult an attorney.

_____

(date)

_____
_____
_____
_____

Dear Sir or Madam:

Please send me any and all forms, instructions, and statutes that are available without charge for forming a **domestic nonprofit corporation**.

Thank you,

This page intentionally left blank.

_____

(date)

_____
_____
_____
_____

Dear Sir or Madam:

Please send me any and all forms, instructions, statutes, and other information necessary for registering and obtaining a tax exemption for a **domestic nonprofit corporation**.

Thank you,

This page intentionally left blank.

_____
(date)

_____
_____
_____
_____

Dear Sir or Madam:

Please send me any and all forms, instructions, statutes, and other information on registration for charitable solicitation in this state for a **domestic nonprofit** corporation.

Thank you,

This page intentionally left blank.

ARTICLES OF INCORPORATION
of

_____

A NONPROFIT CORPORATION

Articles of Incorporation of the undersigned, a majority of whom are citizens of the United States, desiring to form a Nonprofit Corporation under the Nonprofit Corporation Law of _____, do hereby certify:

Article 1: The name of the corporation shall be:

Article 2: The Place in this state where the principal office of the Corporation is to be initially located is the City of _____, _____ County.

Article 3: Said corporation is organized exclusively for charitable, religious, educational, and scientific purposes, including, for such purposes, the making of distributions to organizations that qualify as exempt organizations under Section 501(c)(3) of the Internal Revenue Code, or the corresponding section of any future tax code. The specific purpose of the corporation is to _____

_____

_____

_____.

Article 4: The corporation shall have _____ directors. The initial directors' name(s) and address(es) is/are:

Article 5: No part of the net earnings of the corporation shall inure to the benefit of or be distributable to its members, trustees, officers, or other private persons, except that the corporation shall be authorized and empowered to pay reasonable compensation for services rendered and to make payments and distributions in furtherance of the purposes set forth in Article 3 hereof. No substantial part of the activities of the corporation shall be the carrying on of propaganda, or otherwise attempting to influence legislation, and the corporation shall not participate in, or intervene in (including the publishing or distribution of statements), any political campaign on behalf of or in opposition to any candidate for public office. Notwithstanding any other provision of these articles, this corporation shall not, except to an insubstantial degree, engage in any activities or exercise any powers that are not in furtherance of the purposes of the corporation.

Article 6: Upon the dissolution of the corporation, assets shall be distributed for one or more exempt purposes within the meaning of Section 501(c)(3) of the Internal Revenue Code, or the corresponding section of any future federal tax code, or shall be distributed to the federal government, or to a state or local government, for a public purpose. Any such assets not so disposed shall be disposed of by a Court of Competent Jurisdiction of the county in which the principal office of the corporation is then located, exclusively for such purposes or to such organizations, as said Court shall determine, which are operated exclusively for such purposes.

Article 7: The registered agent and registered office of this corporation are:

Article 8: The corporation ☐ shall ☐ shall not have members. The classes, qualifications, rights and obligations of the members of the corporation (if any) are spelled out in the Bylaws of the corporation.

Article 9: The period of duration of the corporation is perpetual.

Article 10: Names and addresses of Incorporators:

Article 11:

In witness whereof, we, the undersigned, have hereunto subscribed our names this _____ day of _____, 20_____.

_____   _____
Incorporator   Incorporator

_____   _____
Incorporator   Incorporator

The undersigned, being the registered (or statutory) agent listed in these Articles of Incorporation hereby accepts the position as such and agrees to act in such capacity. The undersigned further represents that he or she is familiar with the obligations of the position and agrees to comply with them.

_____
Registered Agent

ADDENDUM TO ARTICLES OF INCORPORATION
of

_____

A NONPROFIT CORPORATION

This Addendum to Articles of Incorporation of the above-named corporation is hereby made a part of said Articles of Incorporation as follows:

Article ___: The Place in this state where the principal office of the Corporation is to be initially located is the City of _____, _____ County.

Article ___: Said corporation is organized exclusively for charitable, religious, educational, and scientific purposes, including, for such purposes, the making of distributions to organizations that qualify as exempt organizations under Section 501(c)(3) of the Internal Revenue Code, or the corresponding section of any future tax code.

Article ___: No part of the net earnings of the corporation shall inure to the benefit of or be distributable to its members, trustees, officers, or other private persons, except that the corporation shall be authorized and empowered to pay reasonable compensation for services rendered and to make payments and distributions in furtherance of the purposes set forth in Article___ of the Articles of the Incorporation. No substantial part of the activities of the corporation shall be the carrying on of propaganda, or otherwise attempting to influence legislation, and the corporation shall not participate in, or intervene in (including the publishing or distribution of statements), any political campaign on behalf of or in opposition to any candidate for public office. Notwithstanding any other provision of these articles, this corporation shall not, except to an insubstantial degree, engage in any activities or exercise any powers that are not in furtherance of the purposes of the corporation.

Article ___: Upon the dissolution of the corporation, assets shall be distributed for one or more exempt purposes within the meaning of Section 501(c)(3) of the Internal Revenue Code, or the corresponding section of any future federal tax code, or shall be distributed to the federal government, or to a state or local government, for a public purpose. Any such assets not so disposed shall be disposed of by a Court of Competent Jurisdiction of the county in which the principal office of the corporation is then located, exclusively for such purposes or to such organizations, as said Court shall determine, which are operated exclusively for such purposes.

This page intentionally left blank.

BYLAWS OF

_____

NONPROFIT CORPORATION

ARTICLE I - OFFICES

The principal office of the Corporation shall be located in the City of _____ and the State of _____. The Corporation may also maintain offices at such other places as the Board of Directors may, from time to time, determine.

ARTICLE II - PURPOSE

Section 1 - Purpose. Said corporation is organized exclusively for charitable, religious, educational, and scientific purposes, including, for such purposes, the making of distributions to organizations that qualify as exempt organizations under Section 501(c)(3) of the Internal Revenue Code, or the corresponding section of any future tax code. The specific purpose of the corporation is to_____

_____

_____

_____

_____

.

Section 2 - No private inurement. No part of the net earnings of the corporation shall inure to the benefit of or be distributable to its members, trustees, officers, or other private persons, except that the corporation shall be authorized and empowered to pay reasonable compensation for services rendered and to make payments and distributions in furtherance of the purposes set forth in Section 1 hereof.

Section 3 - No lobbying. No substantial part of the activities of the corporation shall be the carrying on of propaganda, or otherwise attempting to influence legislation, and the corporation shall not participate in, or intervene in (including the publishing or distribution of statements) any political campaign on behalf of or in opposition to any candidate for public office. Notwithstanding any other provision of these articles, this corporation shall not, except to an insubstantial degree, engage in any activities or exercise any powers that are not in furtherance of the purposes of the corporation

Section 4 - Dissolution. Upon the dissolution of the corporation, assets shall be distributed for one or more exempt purposes within the meaning of Section 501(c)(3) of the Internal Revenue Code, or the corresponding section of any future federal tax code, or shall be distributed to the federal government, or to a state or local government, for a public purpose. Any such assets not so disposed shall be disposed of by a Court of Competent Jurisdiction of the county in which the principal office of the corporation is then located, exclusively for such purposes or to such

Section 5 - Private Foundation. In the event that the Corporation fails to qualify as a public charity under federal tax law and is considered a private foundation, the corporation shall comply with the following: a) It will distribute its income for each tax year at such time and in such manner so that it will not become subject to the tax on undistributed taxable income imposed by section 4942 of the Internal Revenue Code, or corresponding provisions of any later federal tax laws; b) It will not engage in any act of self-dealing as defined in section 4941(d) of the Internal Revenue Code, or corresponding provisions of any later federal tax laws; c) It will not retain any excess business holdings as defined in section 4943(c) of the Internal Revenue Code, or corresponding provisions of any later federal tax laws; d) It will not make any investments in a manner that would subject it to tax under section 4944 of the Internal Revenue Code, or corresponding provisions of any later federal tax laws; and e) It will not make any taxable expenditures as defined in section 4945(d) of the Internal Revenue Code, or corresponding provisions of any later federal tax laws.

ARTICLE III - MEMBERS

Section 1 - Members. The corporation ☐ shall ☐ shall not have members.

Section 2 - Membership Provisions. If the corporation has members, the terms and conditions of membership shall be set out in an Addendum to these Bylaws.

ARTICLE IV - BOARD OF DIRECTORS

Section 1 - Number, Election and Term of Office. The number of the directors of the Corporation shall be _____. This number may be increased or decreased by the amendment of these bylaws by the Board but shall in no case be less than ____ director(s). The Board of Directors shall be elected each year. If this corporation has no members then the Board shall be elected by a majority of the votes of the then current Board. If the corporation has members then the Board shall be elected by the members at their annual meeting. Each director shall hold office until the next annual meeting, and until his successor is elected and qualified, or until his prior death, resignation, or removal.

Section 2 - Vacancies. Any vacancy in the Board shall be filled for the unexpired portion of the term by a majority vote of the remaining directors at any regular meeting or special meeting of the Board called for that purpose.

Section 3 - Duties and Powers. The Board shall be responsible for the control and management of the affairs, property, and interests of the Corporation and may exercise all powers of the Corporation, except as limited by statute.

Section 4 - Annual Meetings. An annual meeting of the Board shall be held on the ____ day of _____ each year unless rescheduled by the Board. The Board from time to time, may provide by resolution for the holding of other meetings of the Board, and may fix the time and place thereof.

Section 5 - Special Meetings. Special meetings of the Board shall be held whenever called by the President or by one of the directors, at such time and place as may be specified in the respective notice or waivers of notice thereof.

Section 6 - Notice and Waiver. Notice of any special meeting shall be given at least five days prior thereto by written notice delivered personally, by mail or by facsimile to each Director at his or her address. If mailed, such notice shall be deemed to be delivered when deposited in the United States Mail with postage prepaid. Any Director may waive notice of any meeting, either before, at, or after such meeting, by signing a waiver of notice. The attendance of a Director at a meeting shall constitute a waiver of notice of such meeting and a waiver of any and all objections to the place of such meeting, or the manner in which it has been called or convened, except when a Director states at the beginning of the meeting any objection to the transaction of business because the meeting is not lawfully called or convened.

Section 7 - Chairman. The Board may, at its discretion, elect a Chairman. At all meetings of the Board, the Chairman of the Board, if any and if present, shall preside. If there is no Chairman, or he or she is absent, then the President shall preside, and in his or her absence, a Chairman chosen by the directors shall preside.

Section 8 - Quorum and Adjournments. At all meetings of the Board, the presence of a majority of the entire Board shall be necessary and sufficient to constitute a quorum for the transaction of business, except as otherwise provided by law, by the Articles of Incorporation, or by these bylaws. A majority of the directors present at the time and place of any regular or special meeting, although less than a quorum, may adjourn the same from time to time without notice, until a quorum shall be present.

Section 9 - Board Action. At all meetings of the Board, each director present shall have one vote. Except as otherwise provided by Statute, the action of a majority of the directors present at any meeting at which a quorum is present shall be the act of the Board. Any action authorized, in writing, by all of the Directors entitled to vote thereon and filed with the minutes of the Corporation shall be the act of the Board with the same force and effect as if the same had been passed by unanimous vote at a duly called meeting of the Board. Any action taken by the Board may be taken without a meeting if agreed to in writing by all members before or after the action is taken and if a record of such action is filed in the minute book.

Section 10 - Telephone Meetings. Directors may participate in meetings of the Board through use of a telephone if such can be arranged so that all Board members can hear all other members. The use of a telephone for participation shall constitute presence in person.

Section 11 - Resignation and Removal. Any director may resign at any time by giving written notice to another Board member, the President, or the Secretary of the Corporation. Unless otherwise specified in such written notice, such resignation shall take effect upon receipt thereof by the Board or by such officer, and the acceptance of such resignation shall not be necessary to make it effective. Any director may be removed for cause by action of the Board.

Section 12 - Compensation. No stated salary shall be paid to directors, as such for their services, but by resolution of the Board a fixed sum and/or expenses of attendance, if any, may be allowed for attendance at each regular or special meeting of the Board. Nothing herein contained shall be construed to preclude any director from serving the Corporation in any other capacity and receiving compensation therefor.

Section 13 - Liability. No director shall be liable for any debt, obligation, or liability of the corporation.

ARTICLE V - OFFICERS

Section 1 - Number, Qualification, Election and Term. The officers of the Corporation shall consist of a President, a Secretary, a Treasurer, and such other officers, as the Board may from time to time deem advisable. Any officer may be, but is not required to be, a director of the Corporation. The officers of the Corporation shall be elected by the Board at the regular annual meeting of the Board. Each officer shall hold office until the annual meeting of the Board next succeeding his or her election, and until his or her successor shall have been elected and qualified, or until his or her death, resignation or removal.

Section 2 - Resignation and Removal. Any officer may resign at any time by giving written notice of such resignation to the President or the Secretary of the Corporation or to a member of the Board. Unless otherwise specified in such written notice, such resignation shall take effect upon receipt thereof by the Board member or by such officer, and the acceptance of such resignation shall not be necessary to make it effective. Any officer may be removed, either with or without cause, and a successor elected by a majority vote of the Board at any time.

Section 3 - Vacancies. A vacancy in any office may, at any time, be filled for the unexpired portion of the term by a majority vote of the Board.

Section 4 - Duties of Officers. Officers of the Corporation shall, unless otherwise provided by the Board, each have such powers and duties as generally pertain to their respective offices as well as such powers and duties as may from time to time be specifically decided by the Board. The President shall be the chief executive officer of the Corporation.

Section 5 - Compensation. The officers of the Corporation shall be entitled to such compensation as the Board shall from time to time determine.

Section 6 - Delegation of Duties. In the absence or disability of any Officer of the Corporation or for any other reason deemed sufficient by the Board of Directors, the Board may delegate his or her powers or duties to any other Officer or to any other Director.

Section 7 - Shares of Other Corporations. Whenever the Corporation is the holder of shares of any other Corporation, any right or power of the Corporation as such shareholder (including the attendance, acting and voting at shareholders' meetings and execution of waivers, consents, proxies, or other instruments) may be exercised on behalf of the Corporation by the President, any Vice President, or such other person as the Board may authorize.

Section 8 - Liability. No officer shall be liable for any debt, obligation, or liability of the corporation.

ARTICLE VI - COMMITTEES

Section 1 - Committees. The Board of Directors may, by resolution, designate an Executive Committee and one or more other committees. Such committees shall have such functions and may exercise such power of the Board of Directors as can be lawfully delegated, and to the extent provided in the resolution or resolutions creating such committee or committees. Meetings of committees may be held without notice at such time and at such place as shall from time to time be determined by the committees. The committees of the corporation shall keep regular minutes of their proceedings, and report these minutes to the Board of Directors when required.

ARTICLE VII - BOOKS, RECORDS AND REPORTS

Section 1 - Annual Report. The President of the Corporation shall cause to be prepared annual or other reports required by law and shall provide copies to the Board of Directors.

Section 2 - Permanent Records. The corporation shall keep current and correct records of the accounts, minutes of the meetings and proceedings and membership records (if any) of the corporation. Such records shall be kept at the registered office or the principal place of business of the corporation. Any such records shall be in written form or in a form capable of being converted into written form.

Section 3 - Inspection of Corporate Records. If this corporation has members, then those members shall have the right at any reasonable time, and on written demand stating the purpose thereof, to examine and make copies from the relevant books and records of accounts, minutes, and records of the Corporation.

ARTICLE VIII - FISCAL YEAR

Section 1 - Fiscal year. The fiscal year of the Corporation shall be the period selected by the Board of Directors as the tax year of the Corporation for federal income tax purposes.

ARTICLE IX - CORPORATE SEAL

Section 1 - Seal. The Board of Directors may adopt, use, and modify a corporate seal. Failure to affix the seal to corporate documents shall not affect the validity of such document.

ARTICLE X - AMENDMENTS

Section 1 - Articles of Incorporation. The Articles of Incorporation may be amended by the Board of Directors unless this corporation has members, in which case they can be amended as provided by law.

Section 2 - Bylaws. These Bylaws may be amended by the Board of Directors

ARTICLE XI - INDEMNIFICATION

Section 1 - Indemnification. Any officer, director, or employee of the Corporation shall be indemnified and held harmless to the full extent allowed by law.

Section 2 - Insurance. The corporation may but is not required to obtain insurance providing for indemnification of directors, officers, and employees.

Certified to be the Bylaws of the corporation adopted by the Board of Directors on _____, 20_____.

_____

                                                                           Secretary

ADDENDUM TO BYLAWS OF

_____

A NONPROFIT CORPORATION

MEMBERS

Section 1 - Members. The corporation shall have one class of members and each member shall have one vote. The Corporation shall keep a list of all active members. Memberships shall not be transferable.

Section 2 - Admission and Termination. Any person may be admitted to membership in the corporation upon payment of such application fee and dues as shall be determined by the board of directors. A member may terminate his or her membership at any time by giving notice to an officer or director of the corporation. The Board of Directors may terminate a member who is delinquent in paying dues or who has acted contrary to the interests of the Corporation. Prior to termination of a member, the Corporation shall give said member thirty (30) days written notice to pay the dues or to explain satisfactorily to the Board alleged to be contrary to the interests of the Corporation.

Section 3 - Annual Meetings. The annual meeting of the members of the Corporation shall be held each year on the _____ day of _____ at the principal office of the Corporation or at such other date and place as the Board may authorize, for the purpose of electing directors, and transacting such other business as may properly come before the meeting.

Section 4 - Special Meetings. Special meetings of the members may be called at any time by the Board, the President, or by the holders of twenty-five percent (25%) of the shares then outstanding and entitled to vote.

Section 5 - Notice of Meetings. Written or printed notice stating the place, day, and hour of the meeting and, in the case of a special meeting, the purpose of the meeting, shall be delivered personally or by mail not less than ten days, nor more than sixty days, before the date of the meeting. Notice shall be given to each Member of record entitled to vote at the meeting. If mailed, such notice shall be deemed to have been delivered when deposited in the United States Mail with postage paid and addressed to the Member at his or her address as it appears on the records of the Corporation.

Section 6 - Waiver of Notice. A written waiver of notice signed by a Member, whether before or after a meeting, shall be equivalent to the giving of such notice. Attendance of a Member at a meeting shall constitute a waiver of notice of such meeting, except when the Member attends for the express purpose of objecting, at the beginning of the meeting, to the transaction of any business because the meeting is not lawfully called or convened.

Section 7 - Quorum. Except as otherwise provided by Statute, or the Articles of Incorporation, at all meetings of Members of the Corporation, the presence at the commencement of such meetings in person or by proxy of a majority of the total membership of the Corporation entitled to vote, but in no event less than one-third of the Members entitled to vote at the meeting, shall constitute a quorum for the transaction of any business. If any Member leaves after the commencement of a meeting, this shall have no effect on the existence of a quorum, after a quorum has been established at such meeting.

Despite the absence of a quorum at any annual or special meeting of members, the members, by a majority of the votes cast by those entitled to vote thereon, may adjourn the meeting. At any such adjourned meeting at which a quorum is present, any business may be transacted at the meeting as originally called as if a quorum had been present.

Section 8 - Voting. Except as otherwise provided by Statute or by the Articles of Incorporation, any corporate action, other than the election of directors, to be taken by vote of the members, shall be authorized by a majority of votes cast at a meeting of Members.

Except as otherwise provided by Statute or by the Articles of Incorporation, at each meeting of Members, active Member of the Corporation shall be entitled to one vote.

Each Member entitled to vote may do so by proxy; provided, however, that the instrument authorizing such proxy to act shall have been executed in writing by the member him- or herself. No proxy shall be valid after the expiration of eleven months from the date of its execution, unless the person executing it shall have specified therein, the length of time it is to continue in force. Such instrument shall be exhibited to the Secretary at the meeting and shall be filed with the records of the corporation.

Any resolution in writing, signed by all of the Members entitled to vote thereon, shall be and constitute action by such Members to the effect therein expressed, with the same force and effect as if the same had been duly passed by unanimous vote at a duly called meeting of Members and such resolution so signed shall be inserted in the Minute Book of the Corporation under its proper date.

Form **SS-4** (Rev. December 2001) Department of the Treasury Internal Revenue Service	**Application for Employer Identification Number** (For use by employers, corporations, partnerships, trusts, estates, churches, government agencies, Indian tribal entities, certain individuals, and others.) ▶ See separate instructions for each line. ▶ Keep a copy for your records.	EIN OMB No. 1545-0003

Type or print clearly.

1 Legal name of entity (or individual) for whom the EIN is being requested

2 Trade name of business (if different from name on line 1)	**3** Executor, trustee, "care of" name

4a Mailing address (room, apt., suite no. and street, or P.O. box)	**5a** Street address (if different) (Do not enter a P.O. box.)
4b City, state, and ZIP code	**5b** City, state, and ZIP code

6 County and state where principal business is located

7a Name of principal officer, general partner, grantor, owner, or trustor	**7b** SSN, ITIN, or EIN

8a **Type of entity** (check only one box)

☐ Sole proprietor (SSN) _____
☐ Partnership
☐ Corporation (enter form number to be filed) ▶ _____
☐ Personal service corp.
☐ Church or church-controlled organization
☐ Other nonprofit organization (specify) ▶ _____
☐ Other (specify) ▶

☐ Estate (SSN of decedent) _____
☐ Plan administrator (SSN) _____
☐ Trust (SSN of grantor) _____
☐ National Guard   ☐ State/local government
☐ Farmers' cooperative   ☐ Federal government/military
☐ REMIC   ☐ Indian tribal governments/enterprises
Group Exemption Number (GEN) ▶ _____

8b If a corporation, name the state or foreign country (if applicable) where incorporated

State	Foreign country

9 **Reason for applying** (check only one box)

☐ Started new business (specify type) ▶ _____
☐ Hired employees (Check the box and see line 12.)
☐ Compliance with IRS withholding regulations
☐ Other (specify) ▶

☐ Banking purpose (specify purpose) ▶ _____
☐ Changed type of organization (specify new type) ▶ _____
☐ Purchased going business
☐ Created a trust (specify type) ▶ _____
☐ Created a pension plan (specify type) ▶ _____

10 Date business started or acquired (month, day, year)	**11** Closing month of accounting year

12 First date wages or annuities were paid or will be paid (month, day, year). **Note:** *If applicant is a withholding agent, enter date income will first be paid to nonresident alien. (month, day, year)* . . . . ▶

13 Highest number of employees expected in the next 12 months. **Note:** *If the applicant does not expect to have any employees during the period, enter "-0-."* . . . . ▶

Agricultural	Household	Other

14 Check **one** box that best describes the principal activity of your business.

☐ Construction   ☐ Rental & leasing   ☐ Transportation & warehousing   ☐ Health care & social assistance   ☐ Wholesale–agent/broker
☐ Real estate   ☐ Manufacturing   ☐ Finance & insurance   ☐ Accommodation & food service   ☐ Wholesale–other   ☐ Retail
                                                                         ☐ Other (specify)

15 Indicate principal line of merchandise sold; specific construction work done; products produced; or services provided.

16a Has the applicant ever applied for an employer identification number for this or any other business? . . . . . ☐ **Yes**   ☐ **No**
Note: *If "Yes," please complete lines 16b and 16c.*

16b If you checked "Yes" on line 16a, give applicant's legal name and trade name shown on prior application if different from line 1 or 2 above.
Legal name ▶ _____   Trade name ▶ _____

16c Approximate date when, and city and state where, the application was filed. Enter previous employer identification number if known.

Approximate date when filed (mo., day, year)	City and state where filed	Previous EIN

Third Party Designee	Complete this section **only** if you want to authorize the named individual to receive the entity's EIN and answer questions about the completion of this form.	
	Designee's name	Designee's telephone number (include area code) ( )
	Address and ZIP code	Designee's fax number (include area code) ( )

Under penalties of perjury, I declare that I have examined this application, and to the best of my knowledge and belief, it is true, correct, and complete.

Applicant's telephone number (include area code) ( )

Name and title (type or print clearly) ▶

Applicant's fax number (include area code) ( )

Signature ▶   Date ▶

For Privacy Act and Paperwork Reduction Act Notice, see separate instructions.   Cat. No. 16055N   Form **SS-4** (Rev. 12-2001)

Do I Need an EIN?

File Form SS-4 if the applicant entity does not already have an EIN but is required to show an EIN on any return, statement, or other document.[1] **See also the separate instructions for each line on Form SS-4.**

IF the applicant...	AND...	THEN...
Started a new business	Does not currently have (nor expect to have) employees	Complete lines 1, 2, 4a-6, 8a, and 9-16c.
Hired (or will hire) employees, including household employees	Does not already have an EIN	Complete lines 1, 2, 4a-6, 7a-b (if applicable), 8a, 8b (if applicable), and 9-16c.
Opened a bank account	Needs an EIN for banking purposes only	Complete lines 1-5b, 7a-b (if applicable), 8a, 9, and 16a-c.
Changed type of organization	Either the legal character of the organization or its ownership changed (e.g., you incorporate a sole proprietorship or form a partnership)[2]	Complete lines 1-16c (as applicable).
Purchased a going business[3]	Does not already have an EIN	Complete lines 1-16c (as applicable).
Created a trust	The trust is other than a grantor trust or an IRA trust[4]	Complete lines 1-16c (as applicable).
Created a pension plan as a plan administrator[5]	Needs an EIN for reporting purposes	Complete lines 1, 2, 4a-6, 8a, 9, and 16a-c.
Is a foreign person needing an EIN to comply with IRS withholding regulations	Needs an EIN to complete a Form W-8 (other than Form W-8ECI), avoid withholding on portfolio assets, or claim tax treaty benefits[6]	Complete lines 1-5b, 7a-b (SSN or ITIN optional), 8a-9, and 16a-c.
Is administering an estate	Needs an EIN to report estate income on Form 1041	Complete lines 1, 3, 4a-b, 8a, 9, and 16a-c.
Is a withholding agent for taxes on non-wage income paid to an alien (i.e., individual, corporation, or partnership, etc.)	Is an agent, broker, fiduciary, manager, tenant, or spouse who is required to file **Form 1042,** Annual Withholding Tax Return for U.S. Source Income of Foreign Persons	Complete lines 1, 2, 3 (if applicable), 4a-5b, 7a-b (if applicable), 8a, 9, and 16a-c.
Is a state or local agency	Serves as a tax reporting agent for public assistance recipients under Rev. Proc. 80-4, 1980-1 C.B. 581[7]	Complete lines 1, 2, 4a-5b, 8a, 9, and 16a-c.
Is a single-member LLC	Needs an EIN to file **Form 8832,** Classification Election, for filing employment tax returns, **or** for state reporting purposes[8]	Complete lines 1-16c (as applicable).
Is an S corporation	Needs an EIN to file **Form 2553,** Election by a Small Business Corporation[9]	Complete lines 1-16c (as applicable).

[1] For example, a sole proprietorship or self-employed farmer who establishes a qualified retirement plan, or is required to file excise, employment, alcohol, tobacco, or firearms returns, must have an EIN. **A partnership, corporation, REMIC (real estate mortgage investment conduit), nonprofit organization (church, club, etc.), or farmers' cooperative must use an EIN for any tax-related purpose even if the entity does not have employees.**

[2] However, **do not** apply for a new EIN if the existing entity only **(a)** changed its business name, **(b)** elected on Form 8832 to change the way it is taxed (or is covered by the default rules), or **(c)** terminated its partnership status because at least 50% of the total interests in partnership capital and profits were sold or exchanged within a 12-month period. (The EIN of the terminated partnership should continue to be used. See Regulations section 301.6109-1(d)(2)(iii).)

[3] Do not use the EIN of the prior business unless you became the "owner" of a corporation by acquiring its stock.

[4] However, IRA trusts that are required to file **Form 990-T,** Exempt Organization Business Income Tax Return, must have an EIN.

[5] A plan administrator is the person or group of persons specified as the administrator by the instrument under which the plan is operated.

[6] Entities applying to be a Qualified Intermediary (QI) need a QI-EIN even if they already have an EIN. **See Rev. Proc. 2000-12.**

[7] See also *Household employer* on page 4. (**Note:** State or local agencies may need an EIN for other reasons, e.g., hired employees.)

[8] Most LLCs **do not** need to file Form 8832. See **Limited liability company (LLC)** on page 4 for details on completing Form SS-4 for an LLC.

[9] An existing corporation that is electing or revoking S corporation status should use its previously-assigned EIN.

✵

Instructions for Form SS-4
(Rev. September 2003)

Department of the Treasury
Internal Revenue Service

For use with Form SS-4 (Rev. December 2001)
Application for Employer Identification Number.

Section references are to the Internal Revenue Code unless otherwise noted.

General Instructions

Use these instructions to complete **Form SS-4,** Application for Employer Identification Number. Also see **Do I Need an EIN?** on page 2 of Form SS-4.

Purpose of Form

Use Form SS-4 to apply for an employer identification number (EIN). An EIN is a nine-digit number (for example, 12-3456789) assigned to sole proprietors, corporations, partnerships, estates, trusts, and other entities for tax filing and reporting purposes. The information you provide on this form will establish your business tax account.

*An EIN is for use in connection with your business activities only. Do **not** use your EIN in place of your social security number (SSN).*

Items To Note

Apply online. You can now apply for and receive an EIN online using the internet. See **How To Apply** below.

File only one Form SS-4. Generally, a sole proprietor should file only one Form SS-4 and needs only one EIN, regardless of the number of businesses operated as a sole proprietorship or trade names under which a business operates. However, if the proprietorship incorporates or enters into a partnership, a new EIN is required. Also, each corporation in an affiliated group must have its own EIN.

EIN applied for, but not received. If you do not have an EIN by the time a return is due, write "Applied For" and the date you applied in the space shown for the number. **Do not** show your SSN as an EIN on returns.

If you do not have an EIN by the time a tax deposit is due, send your payment to the Internal Revenue Service Center for your filing area as shown in the instructions for the form that you are filing. Make your check or money order payable to the "United States Treasury" and show your name (as shown on Form SS-4), address, type of tax, period covered, and date you applied for an EIN.

How To Apply

You can apply for an EIN online, by telephone, by fax, or by mail depending on how soon you need to use the EIN. Use only one method for each entity so you do not receive more than one EIN for an entity.

Online. You can receive your EIN by internet and use it immediately to file a return or make a payment. Go to the

IRS website at **www.irs.gov/businesses** and click on **Employer ID Numbers** under **topics.**

Telephone. You can receive your EIN by telephone and use it immediately to file a return or make a payment. Call the IRS at **1-800-829-4933.** (International applicants must call 215-516-6999.) The hours of operation are 7:00 a.m. to 10:00 p.m. The person making the call must be authorized to sign the form or be an authorized designee. See **Signature** and **Third Party Designee** on page 6. Also see the **TIP** below.

If you are applying by telephone, it will be helpful to complete Form SS-4 before contacting the IRS. An IRS representative will use the information from the Form SS-4 to establish your account and assign you an EIN. Write the number you are given on the upper right corner of the form and sign and date it. Keep this copy for your records.

If requested by an IRS representative, mail or fax (facsimile) the signed Form SS-4 (including any Third Party Designee authorization) within 24 hours to the IRS address provided by the IRS representative.

*Taxpayer representatives can apply for an EIN on behalf of their client and request that the EIN be faxed to their **client** on the same day. **Note:** By using this procedure, you are authorizing the IRS to fax the EIN without a cover sheet.*

Fax. Under the Fax-TIN program, you can receive your EIN by fax within 4 business days. Complete and fax Form SS-4 to the IRS using the Fax-TIN number listed on page 2 for your state. A long-distance charge to callers outside of the local calling area will apply. Fax-TIN numbers can only be used to apply for an EIN. **The numbers may change without notice.** Fax-TIN is available 24 hours a day, 7 days a week.

Be sure to provide your fax number so the IRS can fax the EIN back to you. **Note:** By using this procedure, you are authorizing the IRS to fax the EIN without a cover sheet.

Mail. Complete Form SS-4 at least 4 to 5 weeks before you will need an EIN. Sign and date the application and mail it to the service center address for your state. You will receive your EIN in the mail in approximately 4 weeks. See also **Third Party Designee** on page 6.

Call 1-800-829-4933 to verify a number or to ask about the status of an application by mail.

Cat. No. 62736F

Where To Fax or File

If your principal business, office or agency, or legal residence in the case of an individual, is located in:	Call the Fax-TIN number shown or file with the "Internal Revenue Service Center" at:
Connecticut, Delaware, District of Columbia, Florida, Georgia, Maine, Maryland, Massachusetts, New Hampshire, New Jersey, New York, North Carolina, Ohio, Pennsylvania, Rhode Island, South Carolina, Vermont, Virginia, West Virginia	Attn: EIN Operation P. 0. Box 9003 Holtsville, NY 11742-9003 Fax-TIN 631-447-8960
Illinois, Indiana, Kentucky, Michigan	Attn: EIN Operation Cincinnati, OH 45999 Fax-TIN 859-669-5760
Alabama, Alaska, Arizona, Arkansas, California, Colorado, Hawaii, Idaho, Iowa, Kansas, Louisiana, Minnesota, Mississippi, Missouri, Montana, Nebraska, Nevada, New Mexico, North Dakota, Oklahoma, Oregon, Puerto Rico, South Dakota, Tennessee, Texas, Utah, Washington, Wisconsin, Wyoming	Attn: EIN Operation Philadelphia, PA 19255 Fax-TIN 215-516-3990
If you have no legal residence, principal place of business, or principal office or agency in any state:	Attn: EIN Operation Philadelphia, PA 19255 Telephone 215-516-6999 Fax-TIN 215-516-3990

How To Get Forms and Publications

Phone. You can order forms, instructions, and publications by phone 24 hours a day, 7 days a week. Call 1-800-TAX-FORM (1-800-829-3676). You should receive your order or notification of its status within 10 workdays.

Personal computer. With your personal computer and modem, you can get the forms and information you need using the IRS website at **www.irs.gov** or File Transfer Protocol at **ftp.irs.gov.**

CD-ROM. For small businesses, return preparers, or others who may frequently need tax forms or publications, a CD-ROM containing over 2,000 tax products (including many prior year forms) can be purchased from the National Technical Information Service (NTIS).

To order **Pub. 1796,** Federal Tax Products on CD-ROM, call **1-877-CDFORMS** (1-877-233-6767) toll free or connect to **www.irs.gov/cdorders.**

Tax Help for Your Business

IRS-sponsored Small Business Workshops provide information about your Federal and state tax obligations.

For information about workshops in your area, call 1-800-829-4933.

Related Forms and Publications

The following **forms** and **instructions** may be useful to filers of Form SS-4:
- **Form 990-T,** Exempt Organization Business Income Tax Return
- **Instructions for Form 990-T**
- **Schedule C (Form 1040),** Profit or Loss From Business
- **Schedule F (Form 1040),** Profit or Loss From Farming
- **Instructions for Form 1041 and Schedules A, B, D, G, I, J, and K-1,** U.S. Income Tax Return for Estates and Trusts
- **Form 1042,** Annual Withholding Tax Return for U.S. Source Income of Foreign Persons
- **Instructions for Form 1065,** U.S. Return of Partnership Income
- **Instructions for Form 1066,** U.S. Real Estate Mortgage Investment Conduit (REMIC) Income Tax Return
- **Instructions for Forms 1120 and 1120-A**
- **Form 2553,** Election by a Small Business Corporation
- **Form 2848,** Power of Attorney and Declaration of Representative
- **Form 8821,** Tax Information Authorization
- **Form 8832,** Entity Classification Election
  For more **information** about filing Form SS-4 and related issues, see:
- **Circular A,** Agricultural Employer's Tax Guide (Pub. 51)
- **Circular E,** Employer's Tax Guide (Pub. 15)
- **Pub. 538,** Accounting Periods and Methods
- **Pub. 542,** Corporations
- **Pub. 557,** Exempt Status for Your Organization
- **Pub. 583,** Starting a Business and Keeping Records
- **Pub. 966,** Electronic Choices for Paying ALL Your Federal Taxes
- **Pub. 1635,** Understanding Your EIN
- **Package 1023,** Application for Recognition of Exemption Under Section 501(c)(3) of the Internal Revenue Code
- **Package 1024,** Application for Recognition of Exemption Under Section 501(a)

Specific Instructions

Print or type all entries on Form SS-4. Follow the instructions for each line to expedite processing and to avoid unnecessary IRS requests for additional information. Enter "N/A" (nonapplicable) on the lines that do not apply.

Line 1—Legal name of entity (or individual) for whom the EIN is being requested. Enter the legal name of the entity (or individual) applying for the EIN exactly as it appears on the social security card, charter, or other applicable legal document.

Individuals. Enter your first name, middle initial, and last name. If you are a sole proprietor, enter your individual name, not your business name. Enter your business name on line 2. Do not use abbreviations or nicknames on line 1.

Trusts. Enter the name of the trust.

Estate of a decedent. Enter the name of the estate.

Partnerships. Enter the legal name of the partnership as it appears in the partnership agreement.

Corporations. Enter the corporate name as it appears in the corporation charter or other legal document creating it.

Plan administrators. Enter the name of the plan administrator. A plan administrator who already has an EIN should use that number.

Line 2—Trade name of business. Enter the trade name of the business if different from the legal name. The trade name is the "doing business as " (DBA) name.

*Use the full legal name shown on line 1 on all tax returns filed for the entity. (However, if you enter a trade name on line 2 and choose to use the trade name instead of the legal name, enter the trade name on **all returns** you file.) To prevent processing delays and errors, **always** use the legal name only (or the trade name only) on **all** tax returns.*

Line 3—Executor, trustee, "care of" name. Trusts enter the name of the trustee. Estates enter the name of the executor, administrator, or other fiduciary. If the entity applying has a designated person to receive tax information, enter that person's name as the "care of" person. Enter the individual's first name, middle initial, and last name.

Lines 4a-b—Mailing address. Enter the mailing address for the entity's correspondence. If line 3 is completed, enter the address for the executor, trustee or "care of" person. Generally, this address will be used on all tax returns.

*File **Form 8822,** Change of Address, to report any subsequent changes to the entity's mailing address.*

Lines 5a-b—Street address. Provide the entity's physical address **only** if different from its mailing address shown in lines 4a-b. **Do not** enter a P.O. box number here.

Line 6—County and state where principal business is located. Enter the entity's primary **physical** location.

Lines 7a-b—Name of principal officer, general partner, grantor, owner, or trustor. Enter the first name, middle initial, last name, and SSN of **(a)** the principal officer if the business is a corporation, **(b)** a general partner if a partnership, **(c)** the owner of an entity that is disregarded as separate from its owner (disregarded entities owned by a corporation enter the corporation's name and EIN), or **(d)** a grantor, owner, or trustor if a trust.

If the person in question is an **alien individual** with a previously assigned individual taxpayer identification number (ITIN), enter the ITIN in the space provided and submit a copy of an official identifying document. If

necessary, complete **Form W-7,** Application for IRS Individual Taxpayer Identification Number, to obtain an ITIN.

You are **required** to enter an SSN, ITIN, or EIN unless the only reason you are applying for an EIN is to make an entity classification election (see Regulations sections 301.7701-1 through 301.7701-3) and you are a nonresident alien with no effectively connected income from sources within the United States.

Line 8a—Type of entity. Check the box that best describes the type of entity applying for the EIN. If you are an alien individual with an ITIN previously assigned to you, enter the ITIN in place of a requested SSN.

*This is not an election for a tax classification of an entity. See **Limited liability company (LLC)** on page 4.*

Other. If not specifically listed, check the "Other" box, enter the type of entity and the type of return, if any, that will be filed (for example, "Common Trust Fund, Form 1065" or "Created a Pension Plan"). Do not enter "N/A." If you are an alien individual applying for an EIN, see the **Lines 7a-b** instructions above.
● **Household employer.** If you are an individual, check the "Other" box and enter "Household Employer" and your SSN. If you are a state or local agency serving as a tax reporting agent for public assistance recipients who become household employers, check the "Other" box and enter "Household Employer Agent." If you are a trust that qualifies as a household employer, you do not need a separate EIN for reporting tax information relating to household employees; use the EIN of the trust.
● **QSub.** For a qualified subchapter S subsidiary (QSub) check the "Other" box and specify "QSub."
● **Withholding agent.** If you are a withholding agent required to file Form 1042, check the "Other" box and enter "Withholding Agent."

Sole proprietor. Check this box if you file Schedule C, C-EZ, or F (Form 1040) and have a qualified plan, or are required to file excise, employment, alcohol, tobacco, or firearms returns, or are a payer of gambling winnings. Enter your SSN (or ITIN) in the space provided. If you are a nonresident alien with no effectively connected income from sources within the United States, you do not need to enter an SSN or ITIN.

Corporation. This box is for any corporation **other than a personal service corporation.** If you check this box, enter the income tax form number to be filed by the entity in the space provided.

*If you entered "1120S" after the "Corporation" checkbox, the corporation **must** file Form 2553 **no later than the 15th day of the 3rd month of the tax year the election is to take effect.** Until Form 2553 has been received and approved, you will be considered a Form 1120 filer. See the Instructions for Form 2553.*

Personal service corp. Check this box if the entity is a personal service corporation. An entity is a personal service corporation for a tax year only if:

154 ◆

● The principal activity of the entity during the testing period (prior tax year) for the tax year is the performance of personal services substantially by employee-owners, and
● The employee-owners own at least 10% of the fair market value of the outstanding stock in the entity on the last day of the testing period.

Personal services include performance of services in such fields as health, law, accounting, or consulting. For more information about personal service corporations, see the Instructions for Forms 1120 and 1120-A and Pub. 542.

Other nonprofit organization. Check this box if the nonprofit organization is other than a church or church-controlled organization and specify the type of nonprofit organization (for example, an educational organization).

*If the organization also seeks tax-exempt status, you **must** file either Package 1023 or Package 1024. See Pub. 557 for more information.*

If the organization is covered by a group exemption letter, enter the four-digit **group exemption number (GEN).** (Do not confuse the GEN with the nine-digit EIN.) If you do not know the GEN, contact the parent organization. Get Pub. 557 for more information about group exemption numbers.

Plan administrator. If the plan administrator is an individual, enter the plan administrator's SSN in the space provided.

REMIC. Check this box if the entity has elected to be treated as a real estate mortgage investment conduit (REMIC). See the Instructions for Form 1066 for more information.

Limited liability company (LLC). An LLC is an entity organized under the laws of a state or foreign country as a limited liability company. For Federal tax purposes, an LLC may be treated as a partnership or corporation or be disregarded as an entity separate from its owner.

By **default,** a domestic LLC with only one member is **disregarded** as an entity separate from its owner and must include all of its income and expenses on the owner's tax return (e.g., **Schedule C (Form 1040)**). Also by default, a domestic LLC with two or more members is treated as a partnership. A domestic LLC may file Form 8832 to avoid either default classification and elect to be classified as an association taxable as a corporation. For more information on entity classifications (including the rules for foreign entities), see the instructions for Form 8832.

*Do not file Form 8832 if the LLC accepts the default classifications above. **However, if the LLC will be electing S Corporation status, it must timely file both Form 8832 and Form 2553.***

Complete Form SS-4 for LLCs as follows:
● A single-member domestic LLC that accepts the default classification (above) does not need an EIN and generally should not file Form SS-4. Generally, the LLC

should use the name and EIN of its **owner** for all Federal tax purposes. However, the reporting and payment of employment taxes for employees of the LLC may be made using the name and EIN of **either** the owner or the LLC as explained in Notice 99-6. You can find Notice 99-6 on page 12 of Internal Revenue Bulletin 1999-3 at **www.irs.gov/pub/irs-irbs/irb99-03.pdf. (Note:** If the LLC applicant indicates in box 13 that it has employees or expects to have employees, the owner (whether an individual or other entity) of a single-member domestic LLC will also be assigned its own EIN (if it does not already have one) even if the LLC will be filing the employment tax returns.)
● A single-member, domestic LLC that accepts the default classification (above) and wants an EIN for filing employment tax returns (see above) or non-Federal purposes, such as a state requirement, must check the "Other" box and write "Disregarded Entity" or, when applicable, "Disregarded Entity—Sole Proprietorship" in the space provided.
● A multi-member, domestic LLC that accepts the default classification (above) must check the "Partnership" box.
● A domestic LLC that will be filing Form 8832 to elect corporate status must check the "Corporation" box and write in "Single-Member" or "Multi-Member" immediately below the "form number" entry line.

Line 9—Reason for applying. Check only **one** box. Do not enter "N/A."

Started new business. Check this box if you are starting a new business that requires an EIN. If you check this box, enter the type of business being started. **Do not** apply if you already have an EIN and are only adding another place of business.

Hired employees. Check this box if the existing business is requesting an EIN because it has hired or is hiring employees and is therefore required to file employment tax returns. **Do not** apply if you already have an EIN and are only hiring employees. For information on employment taxes (e.g., for family members), see Circular E.

You may be required to make electronic deposits of all depository taxes (such as employment tax, excise tax, and corporate income tax) using the Electronic Federal Tax Payment System (EFTPS). See section 11, Depositing Taxes, of Circular E and Pub. 966.

Created a pension plan. Check this box if you have created a pension plan and need an EIN for reporting purposes. Also, enter the type of plan in the space provided.

Check this box if you are applying for a trust EIN when a new pension plan is established. In addition, check the "Other" box in line 8a and write "Created a Pension Plan" in the space provided.

Banking purpose. Check this box if you are requesting an EIN for banking purposes only, and enter the banking purpose (for example, a bowling league for depositing dues or an investment club for dividend and interest reporting).

Changed type of organization. Check this box if the business is changing its type of organization. For example, the business was a sole proprietorship and has been incorporated or has become a partnership. If you check this box, specify in the space provided (including available space immediately below) the type of change made. For example, "From Sole Proprietorship to Partnership."

Purchased going business. Check this box if you purchased an existing business. **Do not** use the former owner's EIN unless you became the "owner" of a corporation by acquiring its stock.

Created a trust. Check this box if you created a trust, and enter the type of trust created. For example, indicate if the trust is a nonexempt charitable trust or a split-interest trust.

Exception. Do **not** file this form for certain grantor-type trusts. The trustee does not need an EIN for the trust if the trustee furnishes the name and TIN of the grantor/owner and the address of the trust to all payors. See the Instructions for Form 1041 for more information.

 Do not check this box if you are applying for a trust EIN when a new pension plan is established. Check "Created a pension plan."

Other. Check this box if you are requesting an EIN for any other reason; and enter the reason. For example, a newly-formed state government entity should enter "Newly-Formed State Government Entity" in the space provided.

Line 10—Date business started or acquired. If you are starting a new business, enter the starting date of the business. If the business you acquired is already operating, enter the date you acquired the business. If you are changing the form of ownership of your business, enter the date the new ownership entity began. Trusts should enter the date the trust was legally created. Estates should enter the date of death of the decedent whose name appears on line 1 or the date when the estate was legally funded.

Line 11—Closing month of accounting year. Enter the last month of your accounting year or tax year. An accounting or tax year is usually 12 consecutive months, either a calendar year or a fiscal year (including a period of 52 or 53 weeks). A calendar year is 12 consecutive months ending on December 31. A fiscal year is either 12 consecutive months ending on the last day of any month other than December or a 52-53 week year. For more information on accounting periods, see Pub. 538.

Individuals. Your tax year generally will be a calendar year.

Partnerships. Partnerships must adopt one of the following tax years:
- The tax year of the majority of its partners,
- The tax year common to all of its principal partners,
- The tax year that results in the least aggregate deferral of income, or
- In certain cases, some other tax year.

See the Instructions for Form 1065 for more information.

REMICs. REMICs must have a calendar year as their tax year.

Personal service corporations. A personal service corporation generally must adopt a calendar year unless:
- It can establish a business purpose for having a different tax year, or
- It elects under section 444 to have a tax year other than a calendar year.

Trusts. Generally, a trust must adopt a calendar year except for the following:
- Tax-exempt trusts,
- Charitable trusts, and
- Grantor-owned trusts.

Line 12—First date wages or annuities were paid or will be paid. If the business has or will have employees, enter the date on which the business began or will begin to pay wages. If the business does not plan to have employees, enter "N/A."

Withholding agent. Enter the date you began or will begin to pay income (including annuities) to a nonresident alien. This also applies to individuals who are required to file Form 1042 to report alimony paid to a nonresident alien.

Line 13—Highest number of employees expected in the next 12 months. Complete each box by entering the number (including zero ("-0-")) of "Agricultural," "Household," or "Other" employees expected by the applicant in the next 12 months. For a definition of agricultural labor (farmwork), see Circular A.

Lines 14 and 15. Check the **one** box in line 14 that best describes the principal activity of the applicant's business. Check the "Other" box (and specify the applicant's principal activity) if none of the listed boxes applies.

Use line 15 to describe the applicant's principal line of business in more detail. For example, if you checked the "Construction" box in line 14, enter additional detail such as "General contractor for residential buildings" in line 15.

Construction. Check this box if the applicant is engaged in erecting buildings or other structures, (e.g., streets, highways, bridges, tunnels). The term "Construction" also includes special trade contractors, (e.g., plumbing, HVAC, electrical, carpentry, concrete, excavation, etc. contractors).

Real estate. Check this box if the applicant is engaged in renting or leasing real estate to others; managing, selling, buying or renting real estate for others; or providing related real estate services (e.g., appraisal services).

Rental and leasing. Check this box if the applicant is engaged in providing tangible goods such as autos, computers, consumer goods, or industrial machinery and equipment to customers in return for a periodic rental or lease payment.

Manufacturing. Check this box if the applicant is engaged in the mechanical, physical, or chemical transformation of materials, substances, or components into new products. The assembling of component parts of manufactured products is also considered to be manufacturing.

Transportation & warehousing. Check this box if the applicant provides transportation of passengers or cargo; warehousing or storage of goods; scenic or sight-seeing transportation; or support activities related to these modes of transportation.

Finance & insurance. Check this box if the applicant is engaged in transactions involving the creation, liquidation, or change of ownership of financial assets and/or facilitating such financial transactions; underwriting annuities/insurance policies; facilitating such underwriting by selling insurance policies; or by providing other insurance or employee-benefit related services.

Health care and social assistance. Check this box if the applicant is engaged in providing physical, medical, or psychiatric care using licensed health care professionals or providing social assistance activities such as youth centers, adoption agencies, individual/family services, temporary shelters, etc.

Accommodation & food services. Check this box if the applicant is engaged in providing customers with lodging, meal preparation, snacks, or beverages for immediate consumption.

Wholesale–agent/broker. Check this box if the applicant is engaged in arranging for the purchase or sale of goods owned by others or purchasing goods on a commission basis for goods traded in the wholesale market, usually between businesses.

Wholesale–other. Check this box if the applicant is engaged in selling goods in the wholesale market generally to other businesses for resale on their own account.

Retail. Check this box if the applicant is engaged in selling merchandise to the general public from a fixed store; by direct, mail-order, or electronic sales; or by using vending machines.

Other. Check this box if the applicant is engaged in an activity not described above. Describe the applicant's principal business activity in the space provided.

Lines 16a-c. Check the applicable box in line 16a to indicate whether or not the entity (or individual) applying for an EIN was issued one previously. Complete lines 16b and 16c **only** if the "Yes" box in line 16a is checked. If the applicant previously applied for **more than one** EIN, write "See Attached" in the empty space in line 16a and attach a separate sheet providing the line 16b and 16c information for each EIN previously requested.

Third Party Designee. Complete this section **only** if you want to authorize the named individual to receive the entity's EIN and answer questions about the completion of Form SS-4. The designee's authority terminates at the time the EIN is assigned and released to the designee. **You must complete the signature area for the authorization to be valid.**

Signature. When required, the application must be signed by **(a)** the individual, if the applicant is an individual, **(b)** the president, vice president, or other principal officer, if the applicant is a corporation, **(c)** a responsible and duly authorized member or officer having knowledge of its affairs, if the applicant is a partnership, government entity, or other unincorporated organization, or **(d)** the fiduciary, if the applicant is a trust or an estate. Foreign applicants may have any duly-authorized person, (e.g., division manager), sign Form SS-4.

Privacy Act and Paperwork Reduction Act Notice. We ask for the information on this form to carry out the Internal Revenue laws of the United States. We need it to comply with section 6109 and the regulations thereunder which generally require the inclusion of an employer identification number (EIN) on certain returns, statements, or other documents filed with the Internal Revenue Service. If your entity is required to obtain an EIN, you are required to provide all of the information requested on this form. Information on this form may be used to determine which Federal tax returns you are required to file and to provide you with related forms and publications.

We disclose this form to the Social Security Administration for their use in determining compliance with applicable laws. We may give this information to the Department of Justice for use in civil and criminal litigation, and to the cities, states, and the District of Columbia for use in administering their tax laws. We may also disclose this information to Federal and state agencies to enforce Federal nontax criminal laws and to combat terrorism.

We will be unable to issue an EIN to you unless you provide all of the requested information which applies to your entity. Providing false information could subject you to penalties.

You are not required to provide the information requested on a form that is subject to the Paperwork Reduction Act unless the form displays a valid OMB control number. Books or records relating to a form or its instructions must be retained as long as their contents may become material in the administration of any Internal Revenue law. Generally, tax returns and return information are confidential, as required by section 6103.

The time needed to complete and file this form will vary depending on individual circumstances. The estimated average time is:

Recordkeeping	6 min.
Learning about the law or the form	22 min.
Preparing the form	46 min.
Copying, assembling, and sending the form to the IRS	20 min.

If you have comments concerning the accuracy of these time estimates or suggestions for making this form simpler, we would be happy to hear from you. You can write to the Tax Products Coordinating Committee, Western Area Distribution Center, Rancho Cordova, CA 95743-0001. **Do not** send the form to this address. Instead, see **How To Apply** on page 1.

Form 8718
(Rev. November 2003)
Department of the Treasury
Internal Revenue Service

User Fee for Exempt Organization Determination Letter Request

▶ Attach this form to determination letter application.
(Form 8718 is NOT a determination letter application.)

For IRS Use Only	OMB No. 1545-1798
	Control number _____
	Amount paid _____
	User fee screener

1 Name of organization	2 Employer Identification Number

Caution: *Do not attach Form 8718 to an application for a pension plan determination letter. Use Form 8717 instead.*

3 Type of request   **Fee**

a ☐ Initial request for a determination letter for:
- An exempt organization that has had annual gross receipts averaging not more than $10,000 during the preceding 4 years, or
- A new organization that anticipates gross receipts averaging not more than $10,000 during its first 4 years ▶ **$150**

Note: *If you checked box 3a, you must complete the Certification below.*

Certification

I certify that the annual gross receipts of ....
                                                                                                     name of organization

have averaged (or are expected to average) not more than $10,000 during the preceding 4 (or the first 4) years of operation.

Signature ▶   Title ▶

b ☐ Initial request for a determination letter for:
- An exempt organization that has had annual gross receipts averaging more than $10,000 during the preceding 4 years or
- A new organization that anticipates gross receipts averaging more than $10,000 during its first 4 years . ▶ **$500**

c ☐ Group exemption letters . . . . ▶ **$500**

Instructions

The law requires payment of a user fee with each application for a determination letter. The user fees are listed on line 3 above. For more information, see Rev. Proc. 2003-8, 2003-1, I.R.B. 236, or latest annual update.

Check the box or boxes on line 3 for the type of application you are submitting. If you check box 3a, you must complete and sign the certification statement that appears under line 3a.

Attach to Form 8718 a check or money order payable to the "United States Treasury" for the full amount of the user fee. If you do not include the full amount, your application will be returned. Attach Form 8718 to your determination letter application.

Generally, the user fee will be refunded only if the Internal Revenue Service declines to issue a determination.

Where To File

Send the determination letter application and Form 8718 to:

Internal Revenue Service
P.O. Box 192
Covington, KY 41012-0192

If you are using express mail or a delivery service, send the application and Form 8718 to:

Internal Revenue Service
201 West Rivercenter Blvd.
Attn: Extracting Stop 312
Covington, KY 41011

Paperwork Reduction Act Notice. We ask for the information on this form to carry out the Internal Revenue laws of the United States. If you want your organization to be recognized as tax-exempt by the IRS, you are required to give us this information. We need it to determine whether the organization meets the legal requirements for tax-exempt status.

You are not required to provide the information requested on a form that is subject to the Paperwork Reduction Act unless the form displays a valid OMB control number. Books or records relating to a form or its instructions must be retained as long as their contents may become material in the administration of any Internal Revenue law. The rules governing the confidentiality of Form 8718 are covered in Code section 6104.

The time needed to complete and file this form will vary depending on individual circumstances. The estimated average time is 5 minutes. If you have comments concerning the accuracy of this time estimate or suggestions for making this form simpler, we would be happy to hear from you. You can write to the Tax Products Coordinating Committee, Western Area Distribution Center, Rancho Cordova, CA 95743-0001. **Do not** send this form to this address. Instead, see **Where To File** above.

Attach Check or Money Order Here

Cat. No. 64728Z   Form **8718** (Rev. 11-2003)

This page intentionally left blank.

WAIVER OF NOTICE
OF THE ORGANIZATION MEETING

OF

_____

    We, the undersigned incorporators named in the articles or certificate of incorporation of the above-named corporation, hereby agree and consent that the organization meeting of the corporation be held on the date and time and place stated below and hereby waive all notice of such meeting and of any adjournment thereof.

Place of meeting: _____

Date of Meeting: _____

Time of meeting: _____

Dated: _____

_____
Incorporator

_____
Incorporator

_____
Incorporator

This page intentionally left blank.

Minutes of the Organizational Meeting of
Incorporators and Directors of

_____

The organization meeting of the above corporation was held on _____,
20_____ at _____ at _____
o'clock ___M.

The following persons were present:

_____

_____

_____

_____

_____

_____

The Waiver of Notice of this meeting was signed by all directors and incorporators named in the Articles of Incorporation and filed in the minute book.

The meeting was called to order by _____ an Incorporator named in the Articles of Incorporation. _____ was nominated and elected Chairman and acted as such until relieved by the president. _____ was nominated and elected temporary secretary, and acted as such until relieved by the permanent secretary.

A copy of the Articles of Incorporation, which was filed with the Secretary of State of the State of _____ on _____, 20_____, was examined by the Directors and Incorporators and filed in the minute book.

The election of officers for the coming year was then held and the following were duly nominated and elected by the Board of Directors to be the officers of the corporation, to serve until such time as their successors are elected and qualified:

President: _____

Vice President: _____

Secretary: _____

Treasurer: _____

The proposed Bylaws for the corporation were then presented to the meeting and discussed. Upon motion duly made, seconded and carried, the Bylaws were adopted and added to the minute book.

A corporate seal for the corporation was then presented to the meeting and upon motion duly made, seconded, and carried, it was adopted as the seal of the corporation. An impression thereof was then made in the margin of these minutes.

The necessity of opening a bank account was then discussed and upon motion duly made, seconded, and carried, the following resolution was adopted:

RESOLVED that the corporation open bank accounts with _____ _____ and that the officers of the corporation are authorized to take such action as is necessary to open such accounts; that the bank's printed form of resolution is hereby adopted and incorporated into these minutes by reference and shall be placed in the minute book; that any ____ of the following persons shall have signature authority over the account:

_____   _____

_____   _____

_____   _____

The tax status of the corporation was then discussed and it was moved, seconded, and carried that the officers of the corporation take the necessary action to:

1.   Obtain an employer tax number by filing form SS-4,

2.   Apply for exemption from taxation under IRC § 501(c)(___).

The expenses of organizing the corporation were then discussed and it was moved, seconded, and carried that the corporation pay in full from the corporate funds the expenses and reimburse any advances made by the incorporators upon proof of payment.

The Directors named in the Articles of Incorporation then tendered their resignations, effective upon the adjournment of this meeting. Upon motion duly made, seconded, and carried, the following named persons were elected as Directors of the corporation, each to hold office until the next election of Directors, and until a successor of each shall have been elected and qualified.

_____

_____

_____

_____

There being no further business before the meeting, on motion duly made, seconded, and carried, the meeting adjourned.

DATED: _____

_____
President

_____
Secretary

This page intentionally left blank.

RESOLUTION TO REIMBURSE EXPENSES
OF

_____

A _____ **CORPORATION**

RESOLVED that the corporation shall reimburse the following parties for the organizational expenses of the organizers of this corporation and that the corporation shall amortize these expenses as allowed by IRS regulations.

Name	Expense	Amount
_____	_____	$_____
_____	_____	$_____
_____	_____	$_____
_____	_____	$_____
_____	_____	$_____

Date:_____

_____

_____

_____

_____

_____

This page intentionally left blank.

BANKING RESOLUTION OF

_____

The undersigned, being the corporate secretary of the above corporation, hereby certifies that on the _____ day of _____, 20___ the Board of Directors of the corporation adopted the following resolution:

RESOLVED that the corporation open bank accounts with _____ _____ and that the officers of the corporation are authorized to take such action as is necessary to open such accounts; that the bank's printed form of resolution is hereby adopted and incorporated into these minutes by reference and shall be placed in the minute book; and that any _____ of the following persons shall have signature authority over the account:

_____   _____

_____   _____

and that said resolution has not been modified or rescinded.

Date: _____

_____

Corporate Secretary

(Seal)

This page intentionally left blank.

WAIVER OF NOTICE OF THE ANNUAL MEETING OF
THE BOARD OF DIRECTORS OF

_____

The undersigned, being all the Directors of the Corporation, hereby agree and consent that an annual meeting of the Board of Directors of the Corporation be held on the _____ day of _____, 20_____ at _____ o'clock _____M. at _____ and do hereby waive all notice whatsoever of such meeting and of any adjournment or adjournments thereof.

We do further agree and consent that any and all lawful business may be transacted at such meeting or at any adjournment or adjournments thereof as may be deemed advisable by the Directors present. Any business transacted at such meeting or at any adjournment or adjournments thereof shall be as valid and legal as if such meeting or adjourned meeting were held after notice.

Date: _____

_____
Director

_____
Director

_____
Director

_____
Director

This page intentionally left blank.

MINUTES OF THE ANNUAL MEETING OF
THE BOARD OF DIRECTORS OF

_____

The annual meeting of the Board of Directors of the Corporation was held on the date and at the time and place set forth in the written waiver of notice signed by the Directors, and attached to the Minutes of this meeting.

The following were present, being all the directors of the Corporation:

_____   _____

_____   _____

The meeting was called to order and it was moved, seconded, and unanimously carried that _____ act as Chairman and that _____ act as Secretary.

The minutes of the last meeting of the Board of Directors, which was held on _____, 20___, were read and approved by the Board.

Upon motion duly made, seconded, and carried, the following were elected officers for the following year and until their successors are elected and qualify:

President: _____
Vice President: _____
Secretary: _____
Treasurer: _____

There being no further business to come before the meeting, upon motion duly made, seconded, and unanimously carried, it was adjourned.

_____
Secretary

Directors:

_____

_____

_____

This page intentionally left blank.

Waiver of Notice of Special Meeting of
the Board of Directors of

_____

    The undersigned, being all the Directors of the Corporation, hereby agree and consent that a special meeting of the Board of Directors of the Corporation be held on the ____ day of _____, 20____ at ____ o'clock ___M. at _____ and do hereby waive all notice whatsoever of such meeting and of any adjournment or adjournments thereof.

    The purpose of the meeting is:

    We do further agree and consent that any and all lawful business may be transacted at such meeting or at any adjournment or adjournments thereof as may be deemed advisable by the Directors present. Any business transacted at such meeting or at any adjournment or adjournments thereof shall be as valid and legal as if such meeting or adjourned meeting were held after notice.

Date: _____

_____
Director

_____
Director

_____
Director

_____
Director

This page intentionally left blank.

MINUTES OF SPECIAL MEETING OF
THE BOARD OF DIRECTORS OF

_____

A special meeting of the Board of Directors of the Corporation was held on the date and at the time and place set forth in the written waiver of notice signed by the directors and attached to the Minutes of this meeting.

The following were present, being all the directors of the Corporation:

_____   _____

_____   _____

The meeting was called to order and it was moved, seconded, and unanimously carried that _____ act as Chairman and that _____ as Secretary.

The minutes of the last meeting of the Board of Directors which was held on _____, 20____ were read and approved by the Board.

Upon motion duly made, seconded, and carried, the following resolution was adopted:

There being no further business to come before the meeting, upon motion duly made, seconded, and unanimously carried, it was adjourned.

_____
Secretary

Directors:

_____

_____

_____

_____

This page intentionally left blank.

CHANGE OF REGISTERED AGENT AND/OR REGISTERED OFFICE

1. The name of the corporation is:

2. The street address of the current registered office is:

3. The new address of the registered office is to be:

4. The current registered agent is:

5. The new registered agent is:

6. The street address of the registered office and the street address of the business address of the registered agent are identical.

7. Such change was authorized by resolution duly adopted by the Board of Directors of the corporation or by an officer of the corporation so authorized by the board of directors.

_____
Secretary

Having been named as registered agent and to accept service of process for the above stated corporation at the place designated in this certificate, I hereby accept the appointment as registered agent and agree to act in this capacity. I further agree to comply with the provisions of all statutes relating to the proper and complete performance of my duties, and am familiar with and accept the obligations of my position as registered agent.

_____
Registered Agent

INDEX

P

patriotism, 7
pension plans, 14
political action committees (PACs), 5, 46
political activities, 10, 12
political campaigning, 46
political campaigns, 14
poverty, 6
preventing cruelty, 7
private foundations, 18, 19, 20, 29, 45, 47
private inurement, 29
private inurement doctrine, 4, 11, 43, 44
private operating foundations, 20
profits, 1
    excess, 44
propaganda, 45
proposed adverse determination, 42
public charity, 18, 19
public safety organizations, 19
public scrutiny, 3
public support test, 18, 19
Publication 526, 22, 53
Publication 557, 18, 20, 22, 28, 38, 39, 40, 53
Publication 561, 22
Publication 578, 29, 38
Publication 598, 22
Publication 892, 42
purposes
    defined, 22
    limited, 3
    permitted, 5

Q

quorum, 14

R

raising money, 49
records, 44, 60
recreational clubs, 18, 41

registered agent, 29
registration, 53, 54, 56
religion, 4, 6, 53
Revenue Procedure 95-21, 58
Revenue Ruling 81-178, 58

S

schools, 7, 18
scientific research, 7
self-dealing, 47
service marks, 27
shareholders, 1
soccer clubs, 7
social clubs, 9, 12, 18, 28, 41, 43
social welfare, 7, 12, 18, 28, 41, 51
start-up procedures, 21
statement of purpose, 17
stock-based nonprofit corporation, 16
stockholders, 16
subsidiaries, 8
substantial part test, 45
support test, 20

T

tax-exempt bonds, 2
taxes
    deductible contributions, 17, 18
    deductions, 51
    donations, 1
    excise, 20
    exemptions, 1, 3, 21, 37, 38
    income, 18
    laws, 3, 4
    private foundations, 20
    returns, 61, 62
    Section 4942, 19
    state exemptions, 42
    withholding, 62, 63
taxpayer identification number, 31, 35
testing for public safety, 7

theater groups, 7
trade associations, 9, 12, 17, 18, 43
trademarks, 24, 25, 26, 27
training, 63
trusts, 13, 14

U

undue profits, 11
unemployment compensation, 63
Uniform Registration Statement, 55, 56
unincorporated associations, 13
universities, 7

V

veterans' organizations, 10, 18, 41

W

Waiver of Notice of Organizational Meeting, 33

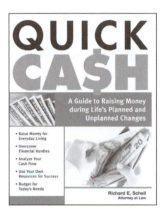
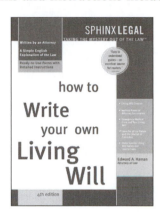
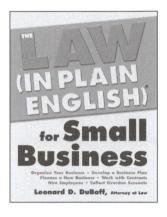

Sphinx® Publishing's National Titles
Valid in All 50 States

LEGAL SURVIVAL IN BUSINESS

The Complete Book of Corporate Forms	$24.95
The Complete Partnership Book	$24.95
The Complete Patent Book	$26.95
Employees' Rights	$18.95
Employer's Rights	$24.95
The Entrepreneur's Internet Handbook	$21.95
The Entrepreneur's Legal Guide	$26.95
How to Form a Limited Liability Company (2E)	$24.95
How to Form a Nonprofit Corporation (2E)	$24.95
How to Form Your Own Corporation (4E)	$26.95
How to Register Your Own Copyright (5E)	$24.95
How to Register Your Own Trademark (3E)	$21.95
Incorporate in Delaware from Any State	$26.95
Incorporate in Nevada from Any State	$24.95
The Law (In Plain English)® for Small Business	$19.95
Most Valuable Business Legal Forms You'll Ever Need (3E)	$21.95
Profit from Intellectual Property	$28.95
Protect Your Patent	$24.95
The Small Business Owner's Guide to Bankruptcy	$21.95
Tax Smarts for Small Business	$21.95

LEGAL SURVIVAL IN COURT

Attorney Responsibilities & Client Rights	$19.95
Crime Victim's Guide to Justice (2E)	$21.95
Grandparents' Rights (3E)	$24.95
Help Your Lawyer Win Your Case (2E)	$14.95
Legal Research Made Easy (3E)	$21.95
Winning Your Personal Injury Claim (2E)	$24.95

LEGAL SURVIVAL IN REAL ESTATE

The Complete Kit to Selling Your Own Home	$18.95
Essential Guide to Real Estate Contracts (2E)	$18.95
Essential Guide to Real Estate Leases	$18.95
Homeowner's Rights	$19.95
How to Buy a Condominium or Townhome (2E)	$19.95
How to Buy Your First Home	$18.95
Working with Your Homeowners Association	$19.95

LEGAL SURVIVAL IN SPANISH

Cómo Hacer su Propio Testamento	$16.95
Cómo Restablecer su propio Crédito y Renegociar sus Deudas	$21.95
Cómo Solicitar su Propio Divorcio	$24.95
Guía de Inmigración a Estados Unidos (3E)	$24.95
Guía de Justicia para Víctimas del Crimen	$21.95
Guía Esencial para los Contratos de Arrendamiento de Bienes Raices	$22.95
Inmigración a los EE. UU. Paso a Paso	$22.95
Inmigración y Ciudadanía en los EE. UU. Preguntas y Respuestas	$16.95
Manual de Beneficios para el Seguro Social	$18.95
El Seguro Social Preguntas y Respuestas	$16.95

LEGAL SURVIVAL IN PERSONAL AFFAIRS

101 Complaint Letters That Get Results	$18.95
The 529 College Savings Plan (2E)	$18.95
The Antique and Art Collector's Legal Guide	$24.95
The Complete Legal Guide to Senior Care	$21.95
Credit Smart	$18.95
Family Limited Partnership	$26.95
Gay & Lesbian Rights	$26.95
How to File Your Own Bankruptcy (5E)	$21.95
How to File Your Own Divorce (5E)	$26.95
How to Make Your Own Simple Will (3E)	$18.95
How to Write Your Own Living Will (4E)	$18.95
How to Write Your Own Premarital Agreement (3E)	$24.95
Law School 101	$16.95
Living Trusts and Other Ways to Avoid Probate (3E)	$24.95
Mastering the MBE	$16.95
Most Valuable Personal Legal Forms You'll Ever Need (2E)	$26.95
The Power of Attorney Handbook (5E)	$22.95
Quick Cash	$14.95
Repair Your Own Credit and Deal with Debt (2E)	$18.95
Sexual Harassment: Your Guide to Legal Action	$18.95
The Social Security Benefits Handbook (3E)	$18.95
Social Security Q&A	$12.95
Teen Rights	$22.95
Traveler's Rights	$21.95
Unmarried Parents' Rights (2E)	$19.95
U.S. Immigration and Citizenship Q&A	$18.95
U.S. Immigration Step by Step (2E)	$24.95
U.S.A. Immigration Guide (5E)	$26.95
The Visitation Handbook	$18.95
The Wills, Estate Planning and Trusts Legal Kit	$26.95
Win Your Unemployment Compensation Claim (2E)	$21.95
Your Right to Child Custody, Visitation and Support (3E)	$24.95

SPHINX® PUBLISHING ORDER FORM

BILL TO:		SHIP TO:	
Phone #	Terms	F.O.B. Chicago, IL	Ship Date

Charge my: ☐ VISA   ☐ MasterCard   ☐ American Express

☐ **Money Order or Personal Check**

Credit Card Number

Expiration Date

Qty	ISBN	Title	Retail	Ext.		Qty	ISBN	Title	Retail	Ext.
		SPHINX PUBLISHING NATIONAL TITLES				____	1-57248-374-1	Law School 101	$16.95	____
____	1-57248-363-6	101 Complaint Letters That Get Results	$18.95	____		____	1-57248-377-6	The Law (In Plain English)® for Small Business	$19.95	____
____	1-57248-361-X	The 529 College Savings Plan (2E)	$18.95	____		____	1-57248-223-0	Legal Research Made Easy (3E)	$21.95	____
____	1-57248-349-0	The Antique and Art Collector's Legal Guide	$24.95	____		____	1-57248-165-X	Living Trusts and Other Ways to	$24.95	____
____	1-57248-347-4	Attorney Responsibilities & Client Rights	$19.95	____				Avoid Probate (3E)		
____	1-57248-148-X	Cómo Hacer su Propio Testamento	$16.95	____		____	1-57248-186-2	Manual de Beneficios para el Seguro Social	$18.95	____
____	1-57248-226-5	Cómo Restablecer su propio Crédito y	$21.95	____		____	1-57248-220-6	Mastering the MBE	$16.95	____
		Renegociar sus Deudas				____	1-57248-167-6	Most Val. Business Legal Forms	$21.95	____
____	1-57248-147-1	Cómo Solicitar su Propio Divorcio	$24.95	____				You'll Ever Need (3E)		
____	1-57248-166-8	The Complete Book of Corporate Forms	$24.95	____		____	1-57248-360-1	Most Val. Personal Legal Forms	$26.95	____
____	1-57248-353-9	The Complete Kit to Selling Your Own Home	$18.95	____				You'll Ever Need (2E)		
____	1-57248-229-X	The Complete Legal Guide to Senior Care	$21.95	____		____	1-57248-388-1	The Power of Attorney Handbook (5E)	$22.95	____
____	1-57248-391-1	The Complete Partnership Book	$24.95	____		____	1-57248-332-6	Profit from Intellectual Property	$28.95	____
____	1-57248-201-X	The Complete Patent Book	$26.95	____		____	1-57248-329-6	Protect Your Patent	$24.95	____
____	1-57248-369-5	Credit Smart	$18.95	____		____	1-57248-385-7	Quick Cash	$14.95	____
____	1-57248-163-3	Crime Victim's Guide to Justice (2E)	$21.95	____		____	1-57248-344-X	Repair Your Own Credit and Deal with Debt (2E)	$18.95	____
____	1-57248-367-9	Employees' Rights	$18.95	____		____	1-57248-350-4	El Seguro Social Preguntas y Respuestas	$16.95	____
____	1-57248-365-2	Employer's Rights	$24.95	____		____	1-57248-217-6	Sexual Harassment: Your Guide to Legal Action	$18.95	____
____	1-57248-251-6	The Entrepreneur's Internet Handbook	$21.95	____		____	1-57248-219-2	The Small Business Owner's Guide to Bankruptcy	$21.95	____
____	1-57248-235-4	The Entrepreneur's Legal Guide	$26.95	____		____	1-57248-168-4	The Social Security Benefits Handbook (3E)	$18.95	____
____	1-57248-346-6	Essential Guide to Real Estate Contracts (2E)	$18.95	____		____	1-57248-216-8	Social Security Q&A	$12.95	____
____	1-57248-160-9	Essential Guide to Real Estate Leases	$18.95	____		____	1-57248-221-4	Teen Rights	$22.95	____
____	1-57248-254-0	Family Limited Partnership	$26.95	____		____	1-57248-366-0	Tax Smarts for Small Business	$21.95	____
____	1-57248-331-8	Gay & Lesbian Rights	$26.95	____		____	1-57248-335-0	Traveler's Rights	$21.95	____
____	1-57248-139-0	Grandparents' Rights (3E)	$24.95	____		____	1-57248-236-2	Unmarried Parents' Rights (2E)	$19.95	____
____	1-57248-188-9	Guía de Inmigración a Estados Unidos (3E)	$24.95	____		____	1-57248-362-8	U.S. Immigration and Citizenship Q&A	$18.95	____
____	1-57248-187-0	Guía de Justicia para Víctimas del Crimen	$21.95	____		____	1-57248-387-3	U.S. Immigration Step by Step (2E)	$24.95	____
____	1-57248-253-2	Guía Esencial para los Contratos de	$22.95	____		____	1-57248-392-X	U.S.A. Immigration Guide (5E)	$26.95	____
		Arrendamiento de Bienes Raices				____	1-57248-192-7	The Visitation Handbook	$18.95	____
____	1-57248-103-X	Help Your Lawyer Win Your Case (2E)	$14.95	____		____	1-57248-225-7	Win Your Unemployment	$21.95	____
____	1-57248-334-2	Homeowner's Rights	$19.95	____				Compensation Claim (2E)		
____	1-57248-164-1	How to Buy a Condominium or Townhome (2E)	$19.95	____		____	1-57248-330-X	The Wills, Estate Planning and Trusts Legal Kit	$26.95	____
____	1-57248-328-8	How to Buy Your First Home	$18.95	____		____	1-57248-138-2	Winning Your Personal Injury Claim (2E)	$24.95	____
____	1-57248-191-9	How to File Your Own Bankruptcy (5E)	$21.95	____		____	1-57248-333-4	Working with Your Homeowners Association	$19.95	____
____	1-57248-343-1	How to File Your Own Divorce (5E)	$26.95	____		____	1-57248-380-6	Your Right to Child Custody,	$24.95	____
____	1-57248-222-2	How to Form a Limited Liability Company (2E)	$24.95	____				Visitation and Support (3E)		
____	1-57248-231-1	How to Form a Nonprofit Corporation (2E)	$24.95	____				**CALIFORNIA TITLES**		
____	1-57248-345-8	How to Form Your Own Corporation (4E)	$26.95	____		____	1-57248-150-1	CA Power of Attorney Handbook (2E)	$18.95	____
____	1-57248-232-X	How to Make Your Own Simple Will (3E)	$18.95	____		____	1-57248-337-7	How to File for Divorce in CA (4E)	$26.95	____
____	1-57248-379-2	How to Register Your Own Copyright (5E)	$24.95	____		____	1-57248-145-5	How to Probate and Settle an Estate in CA	$26.95	____
____	1-57248-104-8	How to Register Your Own Trademark (3E)	$21.95	____		____	1-57248-336-9	How to Start a Business in CA (2E)	$21.95	____
____	1-57248-394-6	How to Write Your Own Living Will (4E)	$18.95	____		____	1-57248-194-3	How to Win in Small Claims Court in CA (2E)	$18.95	____
____	1-57248-156-0	How to Write Your Own	$24.95	____		____	1-57248-246-X	Make Your Own CA Will	$18.95	____
		Premarital Agreement (3E)				____	1-57248-397-0	The Landlord's Legal Guide in CA (2E)	$24.95	____
____	1-57248-230-3	Incorporate in Delaware from Any State	$26.95	____		____	1-57248-241-9	Tenants' Rights in CA	$21.95	____
____	1-57248-158-7	Incorporate in Nevada from Any State	$24.95	____		____	**Form Continued on Following Page**		**SubTotal**	____
____	1-57248-250-8	Inmigración a los EE.UU. Paso a Paso	$22.95	____						
____	1-57248-400-4	Inmigración y Ciudadanía en los EE.UU.	$16.95	____						
		Preguntas y Respuestas								

To order, call Sourcebooks at 1-800-432-7444 or FAX (630) 961-2168 (Bookstores, libraries, wholesalers—please call for discount)

Prices are subject to change without notice.

Find more legal information at: **www.SphinxLegal.com**

SPHINX® PUBLISHING ORDER FORM

Qty	ISBN	Title	Retail	Ext.
		FLORIDA TITLES		
____	1-57071-363-4	Florida Power of Attorney Handbook (2E)	$16.95	____
____	1-57248-396-2	How to File for Divorce in FL (8E)	$28.95	____
____	1-57248-356-3	How to Form a Corporation in FL (6E)	$24.95	____
____	1-57248-203-6	How to Form a Limited Liability Co. in FL (2E)	$24.95	____
____	1-57071-401-0	How to Form a Partnership in FL	$22.95	____
____	1-57248-113-7	How to Make a FL Will (6E)	$16.95	____
____	1-57248-088-2	How to Modify Your FL Divorce Judgment (4E)	$24.95	____
____	1-57248-354-7	How to Probate and Settle an Estate in FL (5E)	$26.95	____
____	1-57248-339-3	How to Start a Business in FL (7E)	$21.95	____
____	1-57248-204-4	How to Win in Small Claims Court in FL (7E)	$18.95	____
____	1-57248-381-4	Land Trusts in Florida (7E)	$29.95	____
____	1-57248-338-5	Landlords' Rights and Duties in FL (9E)	$22.95	____
		GEORGIA TITLES		
____	1-57248-340-7	How to File for Divorce in GA (5E)	$21.95	____
____	1-57248-180-3	How to Make a GA Will (4E)	$16.95	____
____	1-57248-341-5	How to Start a Business in Georgia (3E)	$21.95	____
		ILLINOIS TITLES		
____	1-57248-244-3	Child Custody, Visitation, and Support in IL	$24.95	____
____	1-57248-206-0	How to File for Divorce in IL (3E)	$24.95	____
____	1-57248-170-6	How to Make an IL Will (3E)	$16.95	____
____	1-57248-247-8	How to Start a Business in IL (3E)	$21.95	____
____	1-57248-252-4	The Landlord's Legal Guide in IL	$24.95	____
		MARYLAND, VIRGINIA AND THE DISTRICT OF COLUMBIA		
____	1-57248-240-0	How to File for Divorce in MD, VA and DC	$28.95	____
____	1-57248-359-8	How to Start a Business in MD, VA or DC	$21.95	____
		MASSACHUSETTS TITLES		
____	1-57248-128-5	How to File for Divorce in MA (3E)	$24.95	____
____	1-57248-115-3	How to Form a Corporation in MA	$24.95	____
____	1-57248-108-0	How to Make a MA Will (2E)	$16.95	____
____	1-57248-248-6	How to Start a Business in MA (3E)	$21.95	____
____	1-57248-398-9	The Landlord's Legal Guide in MA (2E)	$24.95	____
		MICHIGAN TITLES		
____	1-57248-215-X	How to File for Divorce in MI (3E)	$24.95	____
____	1-57248-182-X	How to Make a MI Will (3E)	$16.95	____
____	1-57248-183-8	How to Start a Business in MI (3E)	$18.95	____
		MINNESOTA TITLES		
____	1-57248-142-0	How to File for Divorce in MN	$21.95	____
____	1-57248-179-X	How to Form a Corporation in MN	$24.95	____
____	1-57248-178-1	How to Make a MN Will (2E)	$16.95	____
		NEW JERSEY TITLES		
____	1-57248-239-7	How to File for Divorce in NJ	$24.95	____
____	1-57248-448-9	How to Start a Business in NJ	$21.95	____
		NEW YORK TITLES		
____	1-57248-193-5	Child Custody, Visitation and Support in NY	$26.95	____
____	1-57248-351-2	File for Divorce in NY	$26.95	____
____	1-57248-249-4	How to Form a Corporation in NY (2E)	$24.95	____
____	1-57248-401-2	How to Make a NY Will (3E)	$16.95	____
____	1-57248-199-4	How to Start a Business in NY (2E)	$18.95	____
____	1-57248-198-6	How to Win in Small Claims Court in NY (2E)	$18.95	____
____	1-57248-197-8	Landlords' Legal Guide in NY	$24.95	____
____	1-57071-188-7	New York Power of Attorney Handbook	$19.95	____

Qty	ISBN	Title	Retail	Ext.
____	1-57248-122-6	Tenants' Rights in NY	$21.95	____
		NORTH CAROLINA TITLES		
____	1-57248-185-4	How to File for Divorce in NC (3E)	$22.95	____
____	1-57248-129-3	How to Make a NC Will (3E)	$16.95	____
____	1-57248-184-6	How to Start a Business in NC (3E)	$18.95	____
____	1-57248-091-2	Landlords' Rights & Duties in NC	$21.95	____
		NORTH CAROLINA AND SOUTH CAROLINA TITLES		
____	1-57248-371-7	How to Start a Business in NC or SC	$24.95	____
		OHIO TITLES		
____	1-57248-190-0	How to File for Divorce in OH (2E)	$24.95	____
____	1-57248-174-9	How to Form a Corporation in OH	$24.95	____
____	1-57248-173-0	How to Make an OH Will	$16.95	____
		PENNSYLVANIA TITLES		
____	1-57248-242-7	Child Custody, Visitation and Support in PA	$26.95	____
____	1-57248-211-7	How to File for Divorce in PA (3E)	$26.95	____
____	1-57248-358-X	How to Form a Cooporation in PA	$24.95	____
____	1-57248-094-7	How to Make a PA Will (2E)	$16.95	____
____	1-57248-357-1	How to Start a Business in PA (3E)	$21.95	____
____	1-57248-245-1	The Landlord's Legal Guide in PA	$24.95	____
		TEXAS TITLES		
____	1-57248-171-4	Child Custody, Visitation, and Support in TX	$22.95	____
____	1-57248-399-7	How to File for Divorce in TX (4E)	$24.95	____
____	1-57248-114-5	How to Form a Corporation in TX (2E)	$24.95	____
____	1-57248-255-9	How to Make a TX Will (3E)	$16.95	____
____	1-57248-214-1	How to Probate and Settle an Estate in TX (3E)	$26.95	____
____	1-57248-228-1	How to Start a Business in TX (3E)	$18.95	____
____	1-57248-111-0	How to Win in Small Claims Court in TX (2E)	$16.95	____
____	1-57248-355-5	The Landlord's Legal Guide in TX	$24.95	____

SubTotal This page _____

SubTotal previous page _____

Shipping — $5.00 for 1st book, $1.00 each additional _____

Illinois residents add 6.75% sales tax _____

Connecticut residents add 6.00% sales tax _____

Total _____

To order, call Sourcebooks at 1-800-432-7444 or FAX (630) 961-2168 (Bookstores, libraries, wholesalers—please call for discount)

Prices are subject to change without notice.

Find more legal information at: **www.SphinxLegal.com**